The Heart of the Buddha's Path

His Holiness the XIV Dalai Lama

Thorsons

Thorsons
An Imprint of HarperCollins*Publishers*
77–85 Fulham Palace Road,
Hammersmith, London W6 8JB

The Thorsons website address is: www.thorsons.com

The Power of Compassion
first published in Great Britain by Thorsons 1995
© His Holiness the XIV Dalai Lama 1995
The Four Noble Truths
first published in Great Britain by Thorsons 1997
© His Holiness the XIV Dalai Lama 1997

This edition published by Thorsons 1999
5 7 9 10 8 6

His Holiness the XIV Dalai Lama asserts the moral right to
be identified as the author of this work

Buddha motif by Rochelle Green

A catalogue record for this book
is available from the British Library

ISBN 0 7225 3932 0

Printed and bound in Great Britain by
Omnia Books Limited, Glasgow

Contents

Preface   vii

The Power of Compassion   1
The Four Noble Truths   129

Preface

His Holiness the Dalai Lama is the head of state and spiritual leader of the Tibetan people. He is also regarded as the world's foremost Buddhist leader and the manifestation of Chenrezig, the Bodhisattva of Compassion.

A scholar and a man of peace, His Holiness the Dalai Lama has travelled the world, not only to raise international awareness of the enormous suffering of the Tibetan people, but also to talk about Buddhism. The text for this book is taken from a series of public lectures given by His Holiness the Dalai Lama in England in 1993 and 1996. In lectures and tours, he disarms audiences with his simplicity, humour and great warmth. Everywhere his message is the same – the importance of love, compassion and forgiveness.

The Power of Compassion, the first part of this combined volume, is based on lectures at Wembley auditorium and was sponsored by The Tibet Foundation, London. The Office of Tibet would like to thank Jane Rasch and Cait Collins for their many hours spent on transcribing the tapes, as well as His Holiness' translator Geshe Thupten Jinpa and Heather Wardle for their work in editing the text.

The Four Noble Truths, the second part of this volume, is based on lectures given at the Barbican in London. It also contains a public talk given by His Holiness at the Free Trade Centre in Manchester. This was organized by Network of Buddhist Organisation UK. Again, thanks are due to Jane Rasch and Cait Collins for transcription. The Office of Tibet would also like to acknowledge Dominique Side and the translator Geshe Thupten Jinpa for editing the text for publication.

Kesang Y Takla (Mrs)
Representative of His Holiness the Dalai Lama in London

The Power of Compassion

A Collection of Lectures by
His Holiness the XIV Dalai Lama

Translated by Geshe Thupten Jinpa

Contents

1 Contentment, Joy and Living Well   5
2 Facing Death and Dying Well   16
3 Dealing with Anger and Emotion   26
4 Giving and Receiving: A Practical Way
  of Directing Love and Compassion   38
5 Interdependence, Inter-connectedness
  and the Nature of Reality   52
6 The Challenge for Humanity:
  An Interfaith Address   69
7 Questions and Answers on Various
  Problems of the Modern Age   73

o n e

Contentment, Joy and Living Well

Concerned people have asked me to talk about certain subjects and about the best way to deal with the different situations of life. I will try to explain these things in such a way that ordinary people can see how to utilize their own potential in order to face unpleasant situations, such as death, and also mental frustrations, such as anger and hatred.

I am a Buddhist and my whole way of training is according to the Buddhist teaching or Buddha *Dharma*. Although I speak from my own experience, I feel that no one has the right to impose his or her beliefs on another person. I will not propose to you that my way is best. The decision is up to you. If you find some point which may be suitable for you, then you can carry out experiments for yourself. If you find that it is of no use, then you can discard it.

The basic fact is that all sentient beings, particularly human beings, want happiness and do not want pain and suffering. On those grounds, we have every right to be happy and to use different methods or means to overcome suffering and to achieve happier lives. These methods, however, should not infringe on the rights of others, nor should they create more suffering for others. It is worthwhile to think seriously about the positive and negative consequences of these methods. You should be aware that there are differences between short-term and long-term interests and consequences. If there is a conflict between the short-term interest and the long-term interest, the long-term interest is more important. Buddhists usually say that there is no absolute and that everything is relative. So we must judge according to the circumstances.

Our experiences and feelings are mainly related to our bodies and our minds. We know from our daily experience that mental happiness is beneficial. For instance, though two people may face the same kind of tragedy, one person may face it more easily than the other due to his or her mental attitude.

I believe that the idea that all human problems can be solved by machines or by matter is wrong. Of course, material facilities are extremely useful. At the same time, it is quite natural that all our problems cannot be solved by material facilities alone. In a material society there is just as much mental unrest and frustration, if not more. This shows us that we are human beings after all. We are not the product of machines and our bodies are different from purely mechanical things. Therefore, we must think seriously about our own inner abilities and deeper values.

I believe that if someone really wants a happy life then it is very important to pursue both internal and external means; in other words, material development and mental development. One could also say 'spiritual development', but when I say 'spiritual' I do not necessarily mean any kind of religious faith. When I use the word 'spiritual' I mean basic human good qualities. These are: human affection, a sense of involvement, honesty, discipline and human intelligence properly guided by good motivation. We have all these things from birth; they do not come to us later in our lives. Religious faith, however, comes later. In this regard, I believe that there are two levels to the various religious teachings. On one level, religious teachings talk about God or the Almighty, or, in Buddhism, about Nirvana and the next life. Yet on a different level, all religious teachings and traditions teach us to be good human beings, to be warm-hearted people. These religious teachings simply strengthen the basic human good qualities which we have from birth.

As humans, we all have the same human potential, unless there is some sort of retarded brain function. The wonderful human brain is the source of our strength and the source of our future, provided we utilize it in the right direction. If we use the brilliant human mind in the wrong way, it is really a disaster. I think human beings are the superior sentient beings on this planet. Humans have the potential not only to create happy lives for themselves, but also to help other beings. We have a natural creative quality and it is very important to realize this.

It is my belief that the human brain and basic human compassion are by nature in some kind of balance. Sometimes, when we grow up, we may neglect human affection and simply concentrate on the human brain, thus losing the balance. It is then that disasters and unwelcome things happen. If we look at different species of mammals, we will see that nature is very important and that it is a forceful factor that creates some sort of balanced way.

With the realization of one's own potential and self-confidence in one's ability, one can build a better world. According to my own experience, self-confidence is very important. That sort of confidence is not a blind one; it is an awareness of one's own potential. On that basis, human beings can transform themselves by increasing the good qualities and reducing the negative qualities. Transformation does not mean 100 per cent change. Without a basis of something to aim for, how do we develop good things? Buddhists call this potential 'Buddha Nature', which is also the fundamental Clear Light nature of the mind.

The fundamental teaching of the Buddha is his teaching on the Four Noble Truths: 1) That there is suffering; 2) that suffering has cause; 3) that there is cessation of suffering; and, finally, that there is a path to such freedom. The underlying principle of this teaching is the universal principle of causality. What becomes important in the understanding of this basic teaching is a genuine awareness of one's own potentials and the need to utilize them to their fullest. Seen in this light, every human action becomes significant.

For example, the smile is a very important feature of the human face. But because of human intelligence, even that good part of human nature can be used in the wrong way, such as sarcastic smiles or diplomatic smiles, which only serve to create suspicion. I feel that a genuine, affectionate smile is very important in our day-to-day lives. How one creates that smile largely depends on one's own attitude. It is illogical to expect smiles from others if one does not smile oneself. Therefore, one can see that many things depend on one's own behaviour.

Now we should talk about our motivation and mental attitude. As I mentioned earlier, the facility which can provide positive things also has the potential for negative things. The important thing is to use human intelligence and judgement, and to be mindful of the benefits for long-term and short-term happiness. Up to a certain point, the body itself is a good indicator. For instance, if some sort of food causes you discomfort one day, then later you will not want to consume that type of food. It seems that at a certain stage the body itself can tell us what is suitable for our well-being and happiness and what is not. For example, on certain days we tend to have a greater wish to eat green salads and certain vegetables, while on other days we may wish to have something else. In a way, these are bodily indications pointing out what is conducive to our constitution and what is not.

While it is very clear, for instance, that when our bodies need more liquid we develop thirst, sometimes our bodies' indications may be confusing. In those instances it is the responsibility of human intelligence to judge what is best. Sometimes your intelligence may oppose your immediate desire because it knows the long-term consequences. Thus, the role of intelligence is to determine the positive and negative potential of an event or factor which could have both positive and negative results. It is the role of intelligence, with the full awareness that is provided by education, to judge and accordingly utilize the potential for one's own benefit or well-being.

If we examine our mental world, we find that there are various mental factors which have both positive and negative aspects. For instance, we can look at two types of mental factors which are quite similar: one is self-confidence and the other is conceit or pride. Both of them are similar in that they are uplifting states of mind which give you a certain degree of confidence and boldness. But conceit and pride tend to lead to more negative consequences, whereas self-confidence tends to lead to more positive consequences. I usually make a distinction between different types of ego. One type of ego is self-cherishing in order to get some benefit for itself, disregarding the rights of others and even taking advantage of others with acts such as killing, stealing and so on. This is the negative ego. Another ego says, 'I must be a good human being. I must serve. I must take full responsibility.' That kind of strong feeling of 'I' or self opposes some of our negative emotions. Unless you have a strong feeling of self-confidence based on a strong self, it is very difficult to do battle with these negative emotions. So there are two types of ego, and wisdom or intelligence makes a distinction. Similarly, we must be able to distinguish between genuine humility and a lack of confidence. One may mistake the two because both of these are sort of slightly humbling mental functions, but one is positive and the other is negative.

Another example of this may be seen if we examine loving kindness and compassion on the one hand, and strong attachment on the other. While both are concerned with an object of endearment, strong attachment tends to lead to negative consequences, whereas love and compassion lead to more positive consequences. Thus two states of mind which show the same basic characteristics can have differing negative and positive results.

Desire is the same. There is both positive and negative desire. I think generally that desire which has proper reasons is positive, whereas desire which has no proper reasons is negative and can lead to problems. Desire is the prime mover in achieving happiness now and for the future. From the Buddhist viewpoint, the attainment of Buddhahood can be achieved only through a certain type of desire. For instance, the Mahayana Buddhist literature mentions two desires or two aspirations. One is the aspiration to be of benefit to all sentient beings and the other is the aspiration to attain fully the Enlightened state for that purpose. Without these two types of aspiration, the attainment of full Enlightenment is not possible. But there are also negative things which result from desire. The antidote to this negative desire is contentment. There are always extremes, but the middle way is the proper way. So if desire pushes you towards the extreme, then your intelligence has the responsibility to check that course and return you to the centre.

The sense of contentment is a key factor for attaining happiness. Bodily health, material wealth and companions and friends are three factors for happiness. Contentment is the key that will determine the outcome of your relations with all three of these factors.

First, with regard to the body, one can see that too much attachment to one's own body sometimes leads to problems. For that reason, Buddhist training looks at the body from a different angle and tries to analyse the nature of the body. To me, thinking along these lines is very useful. I think about the source of my body and the very nature of blood, bones and flesh. The body is not something pure. Even the act of birth is bloody. Also, no matter how beautiful or polished your body appears on the outside, inside there are still a lot of dirty things. With the covering of skin, the human body sometimes looks very beautiful. But if you look more closely, then this body is really quite horrible! Even though we consume good food, with a nice colour, taste and smell, the food is transformed into dirty things. Yet if we try to remove these dirty aspects of the body we cannot survive. And this is the case not only for other people's bodies, but one's own body too. Most importantly, it is because of our bodies that we have illness, old age, pain and death. Yet despite these faults, the body is very precious because of intelligence, which we can use for many great works. Thus, when one's desire or attachment to one's body becomes extreme, it is very effective to meditate on the impure aspects of the body, particularly to reflect on its source, its constitution and its functions, so that one will have a more realistic and moderate outlook on the body.

Similarly, when our attitude towards our material possessions and wealth is not proper, it can lead to an extreme attachment towards such things as our property, houses and belongings. This can lead to an inability to feel contented. If that happens, then one will always remain in a state of dissatisfaction, always wanting more. In a way, one is then really poor, because the suffering of poverty is the suffering of wanting something and feeling the lack of it. So even though one may have a lot of material possessions, if one is mentally poor, then one will always feel lacking and will always want more.

On the other hand, material facilities are quite crucial for society, because when individuals acquire material possessions and develop materially, it contributes in a way to the well-being of the society and the community. For that you need a certain degree of what I would call healthy competition, because without competition perhaps there might not be such good progress and material development. But it is still quite important to be aware of what type of competition we need, which is a sort of friendly competition that would not seek the destruction or the downfall of rivals or other people, but rather would act as a stimulating factor for growth and progress.

Personally, I can see some parallels to the need for competition in material development in spiritual development in Buddhism. In Buddhism, the foundation of the path is taking refuge in the Three Jewels: the Buddha, the *Dharma* and the *sangha* (the spiritual community). The Buddha, being a fully Enlightened being, is very difficult to emulate. You may draw inspiration from the example of the Buddha, but you can't really compete with him, whereas when you take refuge in the *sangha*, the spiritual community, within the community there may be spiritual companions who are at the very beginning of the path to Enlightenment. When you reflect upon the qualities of the *sangha*, then you can get a sense of encouragement – you feel as if you can compete with the others. This is not really a negative competition; it is a healthy competition. Also, you can emulate the example of others ahead of you, with the confidence that you can reach their stage.

Now when we talk about objects of enjoyment or desire and material well-being, Buddhist literature mentions five types of object of desire: form, sound, odours, tastes and tactile sensations. Whether or not these objects of enjoyment give rise to happiness, satisfaction and contentment, or, conversely, give rise to suffering and dissatisfaction depends very much on how you apply your faculty of intelligence.

Similarly, just as in the case of material objects, one's relations to one's friends and companions have different potentials. In some cases, a certain type of interaction with one's friends or companions could lead to additional suffering, frustration and dissatisfaction. A certain type of interaction can also lead to satisfaction, a sense of fulfilment and happiness. Again, the outcome of our interactions depends upon the application of intelligence.

Another important issue is sexual relations. Sexual relations are part of nature and without them there would be no more human beings – that is clear. But to go to the extreme, to a sort of blind love, often creates problems and more misery. I think the main purpose of sexual relations is reproduction, the creation of beautiful new young babies. One must not have just the desire for sexual pleasure, but also a sense of responsibility, a sense of commitment. If we look at other species, I think some are very admirable. For example, certain birds, such as swans, base their relationships solely on a sense of responsibility and they mate for life. This is very beautiful! Some other animals, like dogs, do not have that kind of responsibility and just enjoy the sexual act, leaving the mother with the entire responsibility. This, I think, is awful!

I think as human beings we must follow nature, but the more civilized manner for sexual relations is not to seek just temporary satisfaction. If one does not see the sense of responsibility and marriage, this is short-sighted. Sometimes people ask me about marriage. Of course I have no experience of it, but I am quite sure about one thing: marriage with too much haste is dangerous. First you must have a long period to examine one another and afterwards, when you have genuine confidence that you can live together, then you should marry. That is the proper way.

It seems that many families in these modern times have problems. On reason is that sexual freedom is too extreme. Moreover, part of your modern culture promotes sex and sexual things and I think this is not very healthy. On the other hand, if we compare sex with violence, then I think sex is better! But often because of sex, violence is also created. I think in reality they are very interlinked.

While the most important thing in family life is children, birth control is also extremely important. Of course, from the Buddhist viewpoint, each individual human life is very precious. From that viewpoint, birth control is not good. But at the same time, the world's population is simply getting too great. Perhaps five billion people can be sustained if all the natural resources are utilized properly, and, according to some scientists, another two or three more billion may be acceptable. But I think it is better if we have a smaller number of people; this is more peaceful and more friendly. With this larger interest then, the conclusion is quite clear that we have to use birth control for the benefit of all humanity. Birth control is very necessary.

So, to repeat, our behaviour in our daily lives is the key factor in determining whether all these facilities and relations really produce genuine, long-lasting satisfaction or not. Much depends on our own attitude. And for this mental factor, motivation is the key thing.

In Buddhist literature, human life is seen as a favourable form of existence or rebirth. There are various factors that could complement the favourable existence as a human being, such as having a long life, good health, material possessions and eloquence so that one can relate to others in a more beneficial way. But as I pointed out earlier, whether or not these conditions can lead to a more beneficial existence or to a more harmful one depends very much on how you utilize them and whether or not you apply the faculty of intelligence.

On that point, Buddhist literature mentions the practice of the Six Perfections. For instance, in the case of acquiring material possessions, according to Buddhism, generosity and the act of giving are seen as causes of wealth. But in order to practise generosity and giving successfully, one must first of all have a sound ethical discipline, a certain type of outlook and principles. And that ethical discipline or those principles can come about only if one has the ability to bear hardships and adverse circumstances when confronted with them. For that, you also need a certain degree of exertion or joyful effort. In order to practise the application of joyful effort successfully, one must have the ability to concentrate, to focus on events, actions or goals. That in turn depends on whether or not you have the ability to exercise your power of judgement, to judge between what is desirable and what is undesirable, what is negative and what is positive. So, in a way, all these Six Perfections are related to the acquisition of even one of the conditions, say, material wealth.

How do we go about implementing in our daily lives these principles which are stipulated in the practice of the Six Perfections? Buddhism recommends living one's life within the ethical discipline of observance of what are known as the Ten Precepts, or Avoidance of the Ten Negative Actions. Out of these Ten Negative Actions, one, known as 'wrong views' or 'perverted views', might make more sense within the context of a religious belief. Other than that, all the other nine Negative Actions are, I would say, common denominators of all religious traditions. They are seen as negative or undesirable for society in general, regardless of any religious point of view.

To conclude, good conduct is the way in which life becomes more meaningful, more constructive and more peaceful. For this, much depends on our own behaviour and our own mental attitude.

two

Facing Death and Dying Well

The issue of facing death in a peaceful manner is a very difficult one. According to common sense, there seems to be two ways of dealing with the problem and the suffering. The first is simply to try to avoid the problem, to put it out of your mind, even though the reality of that problem is still there and it is not minimized. Another way of dealing with this issue is to look directly at the problem and analyse it, make it familiar to you and make it clear that it is a part of all our lives.

I have already touched on the topic of the body and illness. Illness happens. It is not something exceptional; it is part of nature and a fact of life. It happens because the body is there. Of course we have every right to avoid illness and pain, but in spite of that effort, when illness happens it is better to accept it. While you should make every effort to cure it as soon as possible, you should have no extra mental burden. As the great Indian scholar Shantideva has said: 'If there is a way to overcome the suffering, then there is no need to worry; if there is no way to overcome the suffering, then there is no use in worrying.' That kind of rational attitude is quite useful.

Now I want to speak about death. Death is a part of all our lives. Whether we like it or not, it is bound to happen. Instead of avoiding thinking about it, it is better to understand its meaning. On the news we often see murders and death, but some people seem to think that death happens only to others, not to themselves. That kind of attitude is wrong. We all have the same body, the same human flesh, and therefore we will all die. There is a big difference, of course, between natural death and accidental death, but basically death will come sooner or later. If from the beginning your attitude is, 'Yes, death is part of our lives', then it may be easier to face.

So there are two distinct approaches to dealing with a problem. One is to simply avoid it by not thinking about it. The other, which is much more effective, is to face it directly so that you are already conscious of it. Generally, there are two types of problem or suffering: with one type, it is possible that, by adopting a certain attitude, one will be able to actually reduce the force and level of suffering and anxiety. However, there could be other types of problem and suffering for which adopting a certain type of attitude and way of thinking may not necessarily reduce the level of suffering, but which would still prepare you to face it.

When unfortunate things happen in our lives there are two possible results. One possibility is mental unrest, anxiety, fear, doubt, frustration and eventually depression, and, in the worst case, even suicide. That's one way. The other possibility is that because of that tragic experience you become more realistic, you become closer to reality. With the power of investigation, the tragic experience may make you stronger and increase your self-confidence and self-reliance. The unfortunate event can be a source of inner strength.

The success of our lives and our futures, as I have said, depends on our individual motivation and determination or self-confidence. Through difficult experiences, life sometimes becomes more meaningful. If you look at people who, from the beginning of their lives, have had everything, you may see that when small things happen they soon lose hope or grow irritated. Others, like the generation of people in England who experienced World War II, have developed stronger mental attitudes as a result of their hardships. I think the person who has had more experience of hardships can stand more firmly in the face of problems than the person who has never experienced suffering. From this angle then, some suffering can be a good lesson for life.

Now is this attitude just a way of deceiving oneself? Personally, I have lost my country and, worse still, in my country there has been a lot of destruction, suffering and unhappiness. I have spent not only the majority of my life but also the best part of my life outside Tibet. If you think of this from that angle alone, there is hardly anything that is positive. But from another angle, you can see that because of these unfortunate things I have had another type of freedom, such as the opportunity of meeting different people from different traditions and also of meeting scientists from different fields. From those experiences my life has been enriched and I have learned many valuable things. So my tragic experiences have also had some valuable aspects.

Looking at problems from these different angles actually lessens the mental burden or mental frustration. From the Buddhist viewpoint, every event has many aspects and naturally one event can be viewed from many, many different angles. It is very rare or almost impossible that an event can be negative from all points of view. Therefore, it is useful when something happens to try to look at it from different angles and then you can see the positive or beneficial aspects. Moreover, if something happens, it is very useful immediately to make a comparison with some other event or with the events of other people or other nations. This is also very helpful in sustaining your peace of mind.

I will now explain, as a Buddhist monk, how to deal with death. Buddha taught the principles of the Four Noble Truths, the first of which is the Truth of Suffering. The Truth of Suffering is taught within the context of three characteristics of existence, the first being impermanence. When talking about the nature of impermanence we must bear in mind that there are two levels. One is the coarse level, which is quite obvious and is the cessation of the continuation of a life or an event. But the impermanent nature which is being taught in relation to the Four Noble Truths refers to the more subtle aspect of impermanence, which is the transitory nature of existence.

Buddha's teaching of the more subtle aspects of the impermanent nature of existence aims at establishing an appreciation of the basic unsatisfactory nature of our existence. If you understand the nature of impermanence correctly, you will understand that it reveals that any existents which are causally produced, that is, which come about as a result of causes and conditions, entirely depend on causes and conditions for their existence.

Not only that, but the very causes and conditions which have produced them also bring about the disintegration and cessation of those very entities. So, within the seed of the cause of events is the seed for their cessation and disintegration. When this is related to the understanding of the impermanent nature of our own aggregates, the body and mind, then here the cause refers to our own ignorant state of mind, which is the root of our existence, and this reveals that our very physical existence, our bodily existence, is very much governed by the force of an ignorant state of mind.

But it is by first reflecting upon the coarser levels of impermanence that one is eventually led to an appreciation of the subtle levels of impermanence. And by this, one will be able to confront and counteract grasping at permanence or eternal existence of one's own identity or self, because it is this grasping at permanence that forces us to cling onto this very 'now-ness' or matters of one's lifetime alone.

19

By releasing the grip of this grasping and enduring within us, we will be in a better position to appreciate the value of working for our future lifetimes.

One of the reasons why awareness of death and impermanence is so crucial in the Buddhist religious practice is that it is considered that your state of mind at the time of death has a very great effect on determining what form of rebirth you might take. Whether it is a positive state of mind or a negative one will have a great effect. Therefore, Buddhist religious practice greatly emphasizes the importance of the awareness of death and impermanence.

Although the main purpose of a high degree of awareness of impermanence is to train oneself so that at the time of death one will be in a virtuous and positive state of mind and will be assured of a positive rebirth, there are other benefits. One of the positive side-effects of maintaining a very high degree of awareness of death is that it will prepare the individual to such an extent that, when the individual actually faces death, he or she will be in a better position to maintain his or her presence of mind. Especially in Tantric Buddhism, it is considered that the state of mind which one experiences at the point of death is extremely subtle and, because of the subtlety of the level of that consciousness, it also has a great power and impact upon one's mental continuum. So in Tantric practices we find a lot of emphasis placed on death-related meditations and also reflections upon the process of death, so that the individual at the time of death not only retains his or her presence of mind, but also is in a position to utilize that subtle state of consciousness effectively towards the realization of the path.

It is because of this that we find many Tantric meditations, technically known as the 'deity yoga meditations' because they are meditations on deities, involve the dissolution process, reflecting upon the dissolution of elements which the individual experiences at the point of death. In fact, from the Tantric perspective, the entire process of existence is explained in terms of the three stages known as 'death', 'the intermediate state' and 'rebirth'. All of these three stages of existence are seen as states or manifestations of the consciousness and the energies that accompany or propel the consciousness, so that the intermediate state and rebirth are nothing other than various levels of the subtle consciousness and energy. An example of such fluctuating states can be found in our daily existence, when during the 24-hour day we go through a cycle of deep sleep, the waking period and the dream state. Our daily existence is in fact characterized by these three stages.

When talking about the distinctions that are made in the Tantric literature between the subtle and gross levels of consciousness and mind, I think it is important to bear in mind what exactly we mean by 'mental consciousness'. Often people get the impression that when we talk about the sixth mental consciousness there is some kind of autonomous type of consciousness which is totally independent from the bodily states and which is, in a way, the equivalent of the soul. But this is a misunderstanding. I personally think that if we were to examine our mental world we would find that most of our mental states and mental functions have direct physical correlates. Not only the sensory consciousness, but also much of what we would call mental consciousness has physiological bases and is intimately linked with the bodily states, just as scientists would say that the brain and nervous system are the primary physiological bases of much of our conscious experience. Therefore, when the bodily states cease, these mental functions also cease.

But the question really is: what makes it possible for certain physical substances or physiological states to give rise to a mental event or a state of awareness? The Buddhist, particularly the Tantric, explanation points towards what is known as the subtle Clear Light state, which can be seen as independent from a physiological base. And it is this Clear Light state of mind which is the most subtle level of consciousness and which, when it interacts with the physiological base, gives rise to all our conscious and cognitive events.

There are certain indications of the existence of what we call the Clear Light state of mind. There are incidents which generally tend to be more possible for religious practitioners. For instance, among the Tibetan community in exile there have been cases where people have been pronounced clinically dead, that is, their brain function has ceased and the brain is dead but the decomposition of the body has not begun, and they remain in that state for days on end. For instance, my own late tutor, Kyabje Ling Rinpoche, remained in that state for 13 days. He was pronounced clinically dead and he had already experienced the death of the brain, but his body remained fresh and did not decompose for 13 days.

Now there must be some explanation for this. The Buddhist explanation is that, during that state, the individual is not actually dead but rather in the process of dying. Buddhists would explain that although the mind–body relationship may have ceased at the grosser, coarse level, it has not ceased at the subtle level. According to particular Tantric literature known as the *Guhyasamaja Tantra*, when an individual goes through the process of death, there is a certain process of dissolution. From that dissolution into the Clear Light state there is a reversal cycle and when that cycle reaches a certain stage, a new life begins that is called the rebirth. Then that rebirth remains and the individual again goes through a process of dissolution. In a way, death is at the intervening stage when the elements dissolve into the Clear Light and from there re-arise in another form. So death is nothing other than these intervening points when the individual's various physiological elements dissolve into the Clear Light point.

As regards the actual dissolution process of the various elements, the literature mentions different stages of dissolution and their accompanying signs. For instance, in the case of the dissolution of the coarser levels of elements, there are both internal and external signs and indications that mark the dissolution. When it comes to the subtle elements, there are only internal signs such as visions and so forth. There has been a growing interest among scientists who are doing research on death in these descriptions of the dissolution processes, particularly the internal and external signs. As a Buddhist, I think it is very important for us to be aware of the scientific investigations that are being undertaken. However, we must be able to distinguish between phenomena which still remain beyond the verification of existing scientific methodology and phenomena which can be seen as being disproved by existing scientific methods and investigation. I would say that if certain phenomena can be seen as being disproved by science, through scientific investigation and scientific methods, I think as Buddhists we will have to respect those conclusions.

As death becomes something familiar to you, as you have some knowledge of its processes and can recognize its external and internal indications, you are prepared for it. According to my own experience, I still have no confidence that at the moment of death I will really implement all these practices for which I have prepared. I have no guarantee! However, sometimes when I think about death I get some kind of excitement. Instead of fear, I have a feeling of curiosity and this makes it much easier for me to accept death. I wonder to what extent I can implement these practices. Of course, my only burden if I die today is, 'Oh, what will happen to Tibet? What about Tibetan culture? What about the six million Tibetan people's rights?' This is my main concern. Otherwise, I feel almost no fear of death. Perhaps I have some kind of blind confidence! So it is good to reduce the fear of death. In my daily practice of prayer I visualize eight different deity yogas and eight different deaths. Perhaps when death comes all my preparation may fail. I hope not!

Anyway, I think that way is mentally very helpful in dealing with death. Even if there is no next life, there is some benefit if it relieves fear. And because there is less fear, one can be more fully prepared. Just as for battle, without preparation there is a good chance you will lose, but if you are fully prepared, there is more chance of defence. If you are fully prepared then, at the moment of death, you can retain your peace of mind. It is peace of mind at the time of death which is the foundation for cultivating the proper motivation and that is the immediate guarantee of a good rebirth, of a better life to come. Particularly for the practitioner of the Maha-anuttarayoga Tantrayana, death is one of the rare opportunities to transform the subtle mind into wisdom.

As to what is in store for us after death, Buddhists talk about three realms of existence, technically known as 'the form realm', 'the formless realm' and 'the desire realm'. Both the form realm and the desire realm have an intervening stage before you take rebirth, known as 'the intermediate state'. What all of this points towards is that although the occasion of death provides us with the best opportunity to utilize our most subtle level of consciousness, transforming it into a path of wisdom, even if we are not able to seize that opportunity effectively, there is an intermediate state which, though grosser than at the time of death, is a lot more subtle than the consciousness at the time of rebirth. So there is another opportunity. And even if we are unable to seize this opportunity, there is rebirth and a continuing cycle.

So in order to seize the wonderful opportunity accorded at the time of death and, after that, during the intermediate state, we need first to train ourselves to be able to utilize those moments. For that,

Buddhism teaches various techniques to enable the individual to apply certain meditative techniques during each of the dream, deep sleep and waking states.

In conclusion, I think at the time of death a peaceful mind is essential no matter what you believe in, whether it is Buddhism or some other religion. At the moment of death, the individual should not seek to develop anger, hatred and so on. That is very important at the conventional level. I think even non-believers see that it is better to pass away in a peaceful manner. It is much happier. Also, for those who believe in heaven or some other concept, it is also best to pass away peacefully with the thought of one's own God or belief in higher forces. For Buddhists and also other ancient Indian traditions which accept the rebirth or karma theory, naturally at the time of death a virtuous state of mind is beneficial.

three

Dealing with Anger and Emotion

Anger and hatred are two of our closest friends. When I was young I had quite a close relationship with anger. Then eventually I found a lot of disagreement with anger. By using common sense, with the help of compassion and wisdom, I now have a more powerful argument with which to defeat anger.

According to my experience, it is clear that if each individual makes an effort then he or she can change. Of course, change is not immediate and it takes a lot of time. In order to change and deal with emotions it is crucial to analyse which thoughts are useful, constructive and of benefit to us. I mean mainly those thoughts which make us calmer, more relaxed and which give us peace of mind, versus those thoughts which create uneasiness, fear and frustration. This analysis is similar to one which we might use for external things, such as plants. Some plants, flowers and fruit are good for us, so we use them and grow them. Those plants which are poisonous or harmful to us, we learn to recognize and even sometimes to destroy.

There is a similarity with the inner world. It is too simplistic to speak about the 'body' and the 'mind'. Within the body there are billions of different particles. Similarly, there are many different thoughts and a variety of states of mind. It is wise to take a close look into the world of your mind and to make the distinction between beneficial and harmful states of mind. Once you can recognize the value of good states of mind, you can increase or foster them.

Buddha taught the principles of the Four Noble Truths and these form the foundation of the Buddha *Dharma*. The Third Noble Truth is cessation. According to Nagarjuna, in this context cessation means the state of mind or mental quality which, through practice and effort, ceases all the negative emotions. Nagarjuna defines true cessation as a state in which the individual has reached a perfected state of mind which is free from the effects of various afflictive and negative emotions and thoughts. Such a state of true cessation is, according to Buddhism, a genuine *Dharma* and therefore is the refuge that all practising Buddhists seek. Buddha becomes an object of refuge, worthy of respect, because Buddha has realized that state. Therefore one's reverence to the Buddha, and the reason one seeks refuge in the Buddha, is not because Buddha was from the beginning a special person, but because Buddha realized the state of true cessation. Similarly, the spiritual community, or *sangha*, is taken as an object of refuge because the members of the spiritual community are individuals who are either already on, or are embarking on, the path leading to that state of cessation.

We find that the true state of cessation can be understood only in terms of a state of mind which is free from, or which has been purified of, negative emotions and thoughts due to the application of antidotes and counter-forces. True cessation is a state of mind and the factors that lead to this are also functions of the mind. Also, the basis on which the purification takes place is the mental continuum. Therefore, an understanding of the nature of the mind is crucial for Buddhist practice. By saying this, I do not mean that everything which exists is simply a reflection or projection of the mind and that apart from the mind nothing exists. But because of the importance of understanding the nature of mind in Buddhist practice, people often describe Buddhism as 'a science of the mind'.

Generally speaking, in Buddhist literature, a negative emotion or thought is defined as 'a state which causes disturbance within one's mind'. These afflictive emotions and thoughts are factors that create unhappiness and turmoil within us. Emotion in general is not necessarily something negative. At a scientific conference which I attended along with many psychologists and neuro-scientists, it was concluded that even Buddhas have emotion, according to the definition of emotion found in various scientific disciplines. So *karuna* (infinite compassion or kindness) can be described as a kind of emotion.

Naturally, emotions can be positive and negative. However, when talking about anger, etc., we are dealing with negative emotions. Negative emotions are those which immediately create some kind of unhappiness or uneasiness and which, in the long run, create certain actions. Those actions ultimately lead to harm to others and this brings pain or suffering to oneself. This is what we mean by negative emotions.

One negative emotion is anger. Perhaps there are two types of anger. One type of anger could be transformed into a positive emotion. For example, if one has a sincere compassionate motivation and concern for someone and that person does not heed one's warning about his or her actions, then there is no other alternative except the use of some kind of force to stop that person's misdeeds. In Tantrayana practice there are meditative techniques which enable the transformation of the energy of anger. This is the reason behind the wrathful deities. On the basis of compassionate motivation, anger may in some cases be useful because it gives us extra energy and enables us to act swiftly.

However, anger usually leads to hatred and hatred is always negative. Hatred harbours ill will. I usually analyse anger on two levels: on the basic human level and on the Buddhist level. From the human level, without any reference to a religious tradition or ideology, we can look at the sources of our happiness: good health, material facilities and good companions. Now from the stand-point of health, negative emotions such as hatred are very bad. Since people generally try to take care of their health, one technique people can use is their mental attitude. Your mental state should always remain calm. Even if some anxiety occurs, as it is bound to in life, you should always be calm. Like a wave, which rises from the water and dissolves back into the water, these disturbances are very short, so they should not affect your basic mental attitude. Though you cannot eliminate all negative emotions, if your basic mental attitude is healthy and calm, it will not be much affected. If you remain calm your blood pressure and so on remains more normal and as a result your health will improve. While I cannot say scientifically why this is so, I believe that my own physical condition is improving as I get older. I have had the same medicine, the same doctor, the same food, so it must be due to my mental state. Some people say to me, 'You must have some kind of special Tibetan medicine.' But I don't!

As I mentioned earlier, when I was young I was quite short-tempered. I would sometimes excuse this by saying that it was because my father was short-tempered, as if it was something genetic. But as time passes, I think that now I have almost no hatred towards anybody, including towards those Chinese who are creating misery and suffering for Tibetans. Even towards them, I really do not feel any kind of hatred.

Some of my close friends have high blood pressure, yet they never come near to having crises in their health and they never feel tired. Over the years I have met some very good practitioners. Meanwhile, there are other friends who have great material comfort yet, when we start to talk, after the initial few nice words, they begin to complain and grieve. In spite of their material prosperity, these people do not have calm or peaceful minds. As a result, they are always worrying about their digestion, their sleep, everything! Therefore it is clear that mental calmness is a very important factor for good health. If you want good health, don't ask a doctor, look within yourself. Try to utilize some of your potential. This even costs less!

The second source of happiness is material facilities. Sometimes when I wake up in the early morning, if my mood is not very good, then when I look at my watch I feel uncomfortable because of my mood. Then on other days, due perhaps to the previous day's experience, when I wake up my mood is pleasant and peaceful. At that time, when I look at my watch I see it as extraordinarily beautiful. Yet it is the same watch, isn't it? The difference comes from my mental attitude. Whether our use of our material facilities provides genuine satisfaction or not depends on our mental attitude.

It is bad for our material facilities if our mind is dominated by anger. To speak again from my own experience, when I was young I sometimes repaired watches. I tried and failed many times. Sometimes I would lose my patience and hit the watch! During those moments, my anger altered my whole attitude and afterwards I felt very sorry for my actions. If my goal was to repair the watch, then why did I hit it on the table? Again you can see how one's mental attitude is crucial in order to utilize material facilities for one's genuine satisfaction or benefit.

The third source of happiness is our companions. It is obvious that when you are mentally calm you are honest and open-minded. I will give you an example. Perhaps 14 or 15 years ago, there was an Englishman named Phillips, who had a close relationship with the Chinese government, including with Chou En Lai and other leaders. He had known them for many years and he was close friends with the Chinese. One time, in 1977 or 1978, Phillips came to Dharamsala to see me. He brought some films with him and he told me about all the good aspects of China. At the beginning of our meeting there was a big disagreement between us, for we held completely different opinions. In his view, the presence of the Chinese in Tibet was something good. In my opinion, and according to many reports, the situation was not good. As usual, I had no particular negative feeling towards him. I just felt that he held these views due to ignorance. With openness, I continued our conversation. I argued that those Tibetans who had joined the Chinese Communist Party as early as 1930 and who had participated in the Sino–Japanese War and had welcomed the Chinese invasion and enthusiastically collaborated with the Chinese Communists did so because they believed that it was a golden opportunity to develop Tibet, from the viewpoint of Marxist ideology. These people had collaborated with the Chinese out of genuine hope. Then around 1956 or 1957 most of them were dismissed from the various Chinese offices, some were imprisoned and others disappeared. Thus I explained that we are not anti-Chinese or anti-Communist. In fact, I sometimes think of myself as a half-Marxist, half-Buddhist. I explained all these different things to him with sincere motivation and openness and after some time his attitude completely changed. This instance gives me some confirmation that even if there is a big difference of opinion, you can communicate on a human level. You can put aside these different opinions and communicate as human beings. I think that is one way to create positive feelings in other people's minds.

Also, I am quite sure that if this Fourteenth Dalai Lama smiled less, perhaps I would have fewer friends in various places. My attitude towards other people is to always look at them from the human level. On that level, whether president, queen or beggar, there is no difference, provided that there is genuine human feeling with a genuine human smile of affection.

I think that there is more value in genuine human feeling than in status and so on. I am just a simple human being. Through my experience and mental discipline, a certain new attitude has developed. This is nothing special. You, who I think have had a better education and more experience than myself, have more potential to change within yourself. I come from a small village with no modern education and no deep awareness of the world. Also, from the age of 15 or 16 I had an unthinkable sort of burden. Therefore each of you should feel that you have great potential and that, with self-confidence and a little more effort, change really is possible if you want it. If you feel that your present way of life is unpleasant or has some difficulties, then don't look at these negative things. See the positive side, the potential, and make an effort. I think that there is already at that point some kind of partial guarantee of success. If we utilize all our positive human energy or human qualities we can overcome these human problems.

So, as far as our contact with fellow human beings is concerned, our mental attitude is very crucial. Even for a non-believer, just a simple honest human being, the ultimate source of happiness is in our mental attitude. Even if you have good health, material facilities used in the proper way and good relations with other human beings, the main cause of a happy life is within. If you have more money you sometimes have more worries and you still feel hungry for more. Ultimately you become a slave of money. While money is very useful and necessary, it is not the ultimate source of happiness. Similarly, education, if not well balanced, can sometimes create more trouble, more anxiety, more greed, more desire and more ambition – in short, more mental suffering. Friends, too, are sometimes very troublesome.

Now you see can how to minimize anger and hatred. First, it is extremely important to realize the negativeness of these emotions in general, particularly hatred. I consider hatred to be the ultimate enemy. By 'enemy' I mean the person or factor which directly or indirectly destroys our interest. Our interest is that which ultimately creates happiness.

We can also speak of the external enemy. For example, in my own case, our Chinese brothers and sisters are destroying Tibetan rights and, in that way, more suffering and anxiety develops. But no matter how forceful this is, it cannot destroy the supreme source of my happiness, which is my calmness of mind. This is something an external enemy cannot destroy. Our country can be invaded, our possessions can be destroyed, our friends can be killed, but these are secondary for our mental happiness. The ultimate source of my mental happiness is my peace of mind. Nothing can destroy this except my own anger.

Moreover, you can escape or hide from an external enemy and sometimes you can even cheat the enemy. For example, if there is someone who disturbs my peace of mind, I can escape by locking my door and sitting quietly alone. But I cannot do that with anger! Wherever I go, it is always there. Even though I have locked my room, the anger is still inside. Unless you adopt a certain method, there is no possibility of escape. Therefore, hatred or anger – and here I mean negative anger – is ultimately the real destroyer of my peace of mind and is therefore my true enemy.

Some people believe that to suppress emotion is not good, that it is much better to let it out. I think there are differences between various negative emotions. For example, with frustration, there is a certain frustration which develops as a result of past events. Sometimes if you hide these negative events, such as sexual abuse, then consciously or unconsciously this creates problems. Therefore, in this case it is much better to express the frustration and let it out. However, according to our experience with anger, if you do not make an attempt to reduce it, it will remain with you and even increase. Then even with small incidents you will immediately get angry. Once you try to control or discipline your anger, then eventually even big events will not cause anger. Through training and discipline you can change.

When anger comes there is one important technique to help you keep your peace of mind. You should not become dissatisfied or frustrated, because this is the cause of anger and hatred. There is a natural connection between cause and effect. Once certain causes and conditions are fully met, it is extremely difficult to prevent that causal process from coming to fruition. It is crucial to examine the situation so that at a very early stage one is able to put a stop to the causal process. Then it does not continue to an advanced stage. In the Buddhist text *Guide to the Bodhisattva Way of Life*, the great scholar Shantideva mentions that it is very important to ensure that a person does not get into a situation which leads to dissatisfaction, because dissatisfaction is the seed of anger. This means that one must adopt a certain outlook towards one's material possessions, towards one's companions and friends, and towards various situations.

Our feelings of dissatisfaction, unhappiness, loss of hope and so forth are in fact related to all phenomena. If we do not adopt the right outlook, it is possible that anything and everything could cause us frustration. For some people even the name of the Buddha could conceivably cause anger and frustration, although it may not be the case when someone has a direct personal encounter with a Buddha. Therefore, all phenomena have the potential to create frustration and dissatisfaction in us. Yet phenomena are part of reality and we are subject to the laws of existence. So this leaves us only one option: to change our own attitude. By bringing about a change in our outlook towards things and events, all phenomena can become friends or sources of happiness, instead of becoming enemies or sources of frustration.

A particular case is that of an enemy. Of course, in one way, having an enemy is very bad. It disturbs our mental peace and destroys some of our good things. But if we look at it from another angle, only an enemy gives us the opportunity to practise patience. No one else provides us with the opportunity for tolerance. For example, as a Buddhist, I think Buddha completely failed to provide us with the opportunity to practise tolerance and patience. Some members of the *sangha* may provide us with this, but otherwise it is quite rare. Since we do not know the majority of the five billion human beings on this earth, therefore the majority of people do not give us an opportunity to show tolerance or patience either. Only those people whom we know and who create problems for us really provide us with a good opportunity to practise tolerance and patience.

Seen from this angle, the enemy is the greatest teacher for our practice. Shantideva argues very brilliantly that enemies, or the perpetrators of harm upon us, are in fact objects worthy of respect and are worthy of being regarded as our precious teachers. One might object that our enemies cannot be considered worthy of our respect because they have no intention of helping us; the fact that they are helpful and beneficial to us is merely a coincidence. Shantideva says that if this is the case then why should we, as practising Buddhists, regard the state of cessation as an object worthy of refuge when cessation is a mere state of mind and on its part has no intention of helping us. One may then say that although this is true, at least with cessation there is no intention of harming us, whereas enemies, contrary to having the intention of helping us, in fact intend to harm us. Therefore an enemy is not an object worthy of respect. Shantideva says that it is this very intention of harming us which makes the enemy very special. If the enemy had no intention of harming us, then we would not classify that person as an enemy, therefore our attitude would be completely different. It is his or her very intention of harming us which makes that person an enemy and because of that the enemy provides us with an opportunity to practise tolerance and patience. Therefore an enemy is indeed a precious teacher. By thinking along these lines you can eventually reduce the negative mental emotions, particularly hatred.

Sometimes people feel that anger is useful because it brings extra energy and boldness. When we encounter difficulties, we may see anger as a protector. But though anger brings us more energy, that energy is essentially a blind one. There is no guarantee that that anger and energy will not become destructive to our own interests. Therefore hatred and anger are not at all useful.

Another question is that if you always remain humble then others may take advantage of you and how should you react? It is quite simple: you should act with wisdom or common sense, without anger and hatred. If the situation is such that you need some sort of action on your part, you can, without anger, take a counter-measure. In fact, such actions which follow true wisdom rather than anger are in reality more effective. A counter-measure taken in the midst of anger may often go wrong. In a very competitive society, it is sometimes necessary to take a counter-measure. We can again examine the Tibetan situation. As I mentioned earlier, we are following a genuinely non-violent and compassionate way, but this does not mean that we should just bow down to the aggressors' action and give in. Without anger and without hatred, we can manage more effectively.

There is another type of practice of tolerance which involves consciously taking on the sufferings of others. I am thinking of situations in which, by engaging in certain activities, we are aware of the hardships, difficulties and problems that are involved in the short term, but are convinced that such actions will have a very beneficial long-term effect. Because of our attitude and our commitment and wish to bring about that long-term benefit, we sometimes consciously and deliberately take upon ourselves the hardships and problems that are involved in the short term.

One of the effective means by which one can overcome the forces of negative emotions like anger and hatred is by cultivating their counter-forces, such as the positive qualities of mind like love and compassion.

four

Giving and Receiving: A Practical Way of Directing Love and Compassion

Compassion is the most wonderful and precious thing. When we talk about compassion, it is encouraging to note that basic human nature is, I believe, compassionate and gentle. Sometimes I argue with friends who believe that human nature is more negative and aggressive. I argue that if you study the structure of the human body you will see that it is akin to those species of mammals whose way of life is more gentle or peaceful. Sometimes I half joke that our hands are arranged in such a manner that they are good for hugging, rather than hitting. If our hands were mainly meant for hitting, then these beautiful fingers would not be necessary. For example, if the fingers remain extended, boxers cannot hit forcefully, so they have to make fists. So I think that means that our basic physical structure creates a compassionate or gentle kind of nature.

If we look at relationships, marriage and conception are very important. As I said earlier, marriage should not be based on blind love or an extreme sort of mad love; it should be based on a knowledge of one another and an understanding that you are suitable to live together. Marriage is not for temporary satisfaction, but for some kind of sense of responsibility. That is the genuine love which is the basis of marriage.

The proper conception of a child takes place in that kind of moral or mental attitude. While the child is in the mother's womb, the mother's calmness of mind has a very positive effect on the unborn child, according to some scientists. If the mother's mental state is negative, for instance if she is frustrated or angry, then it is very harmful to the healthy development of the unborn child. One scientist has told me that the first few weeks after birth is the most important period, for during that time the child's brain is enlarging. During that period, the mother's touch or that of someone who is acting like a mother is crucial. This shows that even though the child may not realize who is who, it somehow physically needs someone else's affection. Without that, it is very damaging for the healthy development of the brain.

After birth, the first act by the mother is to give the child nourishing milk. If the mother lacks affection or kind feelings for the child, then the milk will not flow. If the mother feeds her baby with gentle feelings towards the child, in spite of her own illness or pain, as a result the milk flows freely. This kind of attitude is like a precious jewel. Moreover, from the other side, if the child lacks some kind of close feeling towards the mother, it may not suckle. This shows how wonderful the act of affection from both sides is. That is the beginning of our lives.

Similarly with education, it is my experience that those lessons which we learn from teachers who are not just good, but who also show affection for the student, go deep into our minds. Lessons from other sorts of teachers may not. Although you may be compelled to study and may fear the teacher, the lessons may not sink in. Much depends on the affection from the teacher.

Likewise, when we go to a hospital, irrespective of the doctor's quality, if the doctor shows genuine feeling and deep concern for us, and if he or she smiles, then we feel OK. But if the doctor shows little human affection, then even though he or she may be a very great expert, we may feel unsure and nervous. This is human nature.

Lastly, we can reflect on our lives. When we are young and again when we are old, we depend heavily on the affection of others. Between these stages we usually feel that we can do everything without help from others and that other people's affection is simply not important. But at this stage I think it is very important to keep deep human affection. When people in a big town or city feel lonely, this does not mean that they lack human companions, but rather that they lack human affection. As a result of this, their mental health eventually becomes very poor. On the other hand, those people who grow up in an atmosphere of human affection have a much more positive and gentle development of their bodies, their minds and their behaviour. Children who have grown up lacking that atmosphere usually have more negative attitudes. This very clearly shows the basic human nature. Also, as I have mentioned, the human body appreciates peace of mind. Things that are disturbing to us have a very bad effect upon our health. This shows that the whole structure of our health is such that it is suited to an atmosphere of human affection. Therefore, our potential for compassion is there. The only issue is whether or not we realize this and utilize it.

The basic aim of my explanation is to show that by nature we are compassionate, that compassion is something very necessary and something which we can develop. It is important to know the exact meaning of compassion. Different philosophies and traditions have different interpretations of the meaning of love and compassion. Some of my Christian friends believe that love cannot develop without God's grace; in other words, to develop love and compassion you need faith. The Buddhist interpretation is that genuine compassion is based on a clear acceptance or recognition that others, like oneself, want happiness and have the right to overcome suffering. On that basis one develops some kind of concern about the welfare of others, irrespective of one's attitude to oneself. That is compassion.

Your love and compassion towards your friends is in many cases actually attachment. This feeling is not based on the realization that all beings have an equal right to be happy and to overcome suffering. Instead, it is based on the idea that something is 'mine', 'my friend' or something good for 'me'. That is attachment. Thus, when that person's attitude towards you changes, your feeling of closeness immediately disappears. With the other way, you develop some kind of concern irrespective of the other person's attitude to you, simply because that person is a fellow human being and has every right to overcome suffering. Whether that person remains neutral to you or even becomes your enemy, your concern should remain because of his or her right. That is the main difference. Genuine compassion is much healthier; it is unbiased and it is based on reason. By contrast, attachment is narrow-minded and biased.

Actually, genuine compassion and attachment are contradictory. According to Buddhist practice, to develop genuine compassion you must first practise the meditation of equalization and equanimity, detaching oneself from those people who are very close to you. Then, you must remove negative feelings towards your enemies. All sentient beings should be looked on as equal. On that basis, you can gradually develop genuine compassion for all of them. It must be said that genuine compassion is not like pity or a feeling that others are somehow lower that yourself. Rather, with genuine compassion you view others as more important than yourself.

As I pointed out earlier, in order to generate genuine compassion, first of all one must go through the training of equanimity. This becomes very important because without a sense of equanimity towards all, one's feelings towards others will be biased. So now I will give you a brief example of a Buddhist meditative training on developing equanimity. You should think about, first, a small group of people whom you know, such as your friends and relatives, towards whom you have attachment. Second, you should think about some people to whom you feel totally indifferent. And third, think about some people whom you dislike. Once you have imagined these different people, you should try to let your mind go into its natural state and see how it would normally respond to an encounter with these people. You will notice that your natural reaction would be that of attachment towards your friends, that of dislike towards the people whom you consider enemies and that of total indifference towards those whom you consider neutral. Then you should try to question yourself. You should compare the effects of the two opposing attitudes you have towards your friends and your enemies, and see why you should have such fluctuating states of mind towards these two different groups of people. You should see what effects such reactions have on your mind and try to see the futility of relating to them in such an extreme manner. I have already discussed the pros and cons of harbouring hatred and generating anger towards enemies, and I have also spoken a little about the defects of being extremely attached towards friends and so on. You should reflect upon this and then try to minimize your strong emotions towards these two opposing groups of people. Then, most importantly, you should reflect on the fundamental equality between yourself and all other sentient beings. Just as you have the instinctive natural desire to be happy and overcome suffering, so do all sentient beings; just as you have the right to fulfil this innate aspiration, so do all sentient beings. So on what exact grounds do you discriminate?

If we look at humanity as a whole, we are social animals. Moreover, the structures of the modern economy, education and so on, illustrate that the world has become a smaller place and that we heavily depend on one another. Under such circumstances, I think the only option is to live and work together harmoniously and keep in our minds the interest of the whole of humanity. That is the only outlook and way we must adopt for our survival.

By nature, especially as a human being, my interests are not independent of others. My happiness depends on others' happiness. So when I see happy people, automatically I also feel a little bit happier than when I see people in a difficult situation. For example, when we see pictures on television which show people starving in Somalia, including old people and young children, then we automatically feel sad, regardless of whether that sadness can lead to some kind of active help or not.

Moreover, in our daily lives we are now utilizing many good facilities, including things like air-conditioned houses. All these things or facilities became possible, not because of ourselves, but because of many other people's direct or indirect involvement. Everything comes together. It is impossible to return to the way of life of a few centuries ago, when we depended on simple instruments, not all these machines. It is very clear to us that the facilities that we are enjoying now are the products of the activities of many people. In 24 hours you sleep on a bed – many people have been involved in that – and in the preparation of your food, too, especially for the non-vegetarian. Fame is definitely a product of other people – without the presence of other people the concept of fame would not even make sense. Also, the interest of Europe depends on America's interest and Western Europe's interest depends on the Eastern European economic situation. Each continent is heavily dependent on the others; that is the reality. Thus many of the things that we desire, such as wealth, fame and so forth, could not come into being without the active or indirect participation and co-operation of many other people.

Therefore, since we all have an equal right to be happy and since we are all linked to one another, no matter how important an individual is, logically the interest of the other five billion people on the planet is more important than that of one single person. By thinking along these lines, you can eventually develop a sense of global responsibility. Modern environmental problems, such as the depletion of the ozone layer, also clearly show us the need for world co-operation. It seems that with development, the whole world has become much smaller, but the human consciousness is still lagging behind.

This is not a question of religious practice, but a question of the future of humanity. This kind of wider or more altruistic attitude is very relevant in today's world. If we look at the situation from various angles, such as the complexity and inter-connectedness of the nature of modern existence, then we will gradually notice a change in our outlook, so that when we say 'others' and when we think of others, we will no longer dismiss them as something that is irrelevant to us. We will no longer feel indifferent.

If you think only of yourself, if you forget the rights and well-being of others, or, worse still, if you exploit others, ultimately you will lose. You will have no friends who will show concern for your well-being. Moreover, if a tragedy befalls you, instead of feeling concerned, others might even secretly rejoice. By contrast, if an individual is compassionate and altruistic, and has the interests of others in mind, then irrespective of whether that person knows a lot of people, wherever that person moves, he or she will immediately make friends. And when that person faces a tragedy, there will be plenty of people who will come to help.

A true friendship develops on the basis of genuine human affection, not money or power. Of course, due to your power or wealth, more people may approach you with big smiles or gifts. But deep down these are not real friends of yours; these are friends of your wealth or power. As long as your fortune remains, then these people will often approach you. But when your fortunes decline, they will no longer be there. With this type of friend, nobody will make a sincere effort to help you if you need it. That is the reality.

Genuine human friendship is on the basis of human affection, irrespective of your position. Therefore, the more you show concern about the welfare and rights of others, the more you are a genuine friend. The more you remain open and sincere, then ultimately more benefits will come to you. If you forget or do not bother about others, then eventually you will lose your own benefit. So sometimes I tell people, if we really are selfish, then wise selfishness is much better than the selfishness of ignorance and narrow-mindedness.

For Buddhist practitioners, the development of wisdom is also very important – and here I mean wisdom which realizes *Shunya*, the ultimate nature of reality. The realization of *Shunya* gives you at least some kind of positive sense about cessation. Once you have some kind of feeling for the possibility of cessation, then it becomes clear that suffering is not final and that there is an alternative. If there is an alternative then it is worth making an effort. If only two of the Buddha's Four Noble Truths exist, suffering and the cause of suffering, then there is not much meaning. But the other two Noble Truths, including cessation, point towards an alternative way of existence. There is possibility of ending suffering. So it is worthwhile to realize the nature of suffering. Therefore wisdom is extremely important in increasing compassion infinitely.

So that is how one engages in the practice of Buddhism: there is an application of the faculty of wisdom, using intelligence, and an understanding of the nature of reality, together with the skilful means of generating compassion. I think that in your daily lives and in all sorts of your professional work, you can use this compassionate motivation.

Of course, in the field of education, there is no doubt that compassionate motivation is important and relevant. Irrespective of whether you are a believer or non-believer, compassion for the students' lives or futures, not only for their examinations, makes your work as a teacher much more effective. With that motivation, I think your students will remember you for the whole of their lives.

Similarly, in the field of health, there is an expression in Tibetan which says that the effectiveness of the treatment depends on how warm-hearted the physician is. Because of this expression, when treatments from a certain doctor do not work, people blame the doctor's character, speculating that perhaps that he or she was not a kind person. The poor doctor sometimes get a very bad name! So in the medical field there is no doubt that compassionate motivation is something very relevant.

I think this is also the case with lawyers and politicians. If politicians and lawyers had more compassionate motivation then there would be less scandal. And as a result the whole community would get more peace. I think the work of politics would become more effective and more respected.

Finally, in my view, the worst thing is warfare. But even warfare with human affection and with human compassion is much less destructive. The completely mechanized warfare that is without human feeling is worse.

Also, I think compassion and a sense of responsibility can also enter into the fields of science and engineering. Of course, from a purely scientific point of view, awful weapons such as nuclear bombs are remarkable achievements. But we can say that these are negative because they bring immense suffering to the world. Therefore, if we do not take into account human pain, human feelings and human compassion, there is no demarcation between right and wrong. Therefore, human compassion can reach everywhere.

I find it a little bit difficult to apply this principle of compassion to the field of economics. But economists are human beings and of course they also need human affection, without which they would suffer. However, if you think only of profit, irrespective of the consequences, then drug dealers are not wrong, because, from the economic viewpoint, they are also making tremendous profits. But because this is very harmful for society and for the community, we call this wrong and name these people criminals. If that is the case, then I think arms dealers are in the same category. The arms trade is equally dangerous and irresponsible.

So I think for these reasons, human compassion, or what I sometimes call 'human affection', is the key factor for all human business. Just as you see that with the palm of our hand all five fingers become useful, if these fingers were not connected to the palm they would be useless. Similarly, every human action that is without human feeling becomes dangerous. With human feeling and an appreciation of human values, all human activities become constructive.

Even religion, which is supposedly good for humanity, without that basic human compassionate attitude can become foul. Unfortunately even now there are problems which are entirely down to different religions. So human compassion is something fundamental. If that is there, then all other human activities become more useful.

Generally speaking, I have the impression that in education and some other areas there is some negligence of the issue of human motivation. Perhaps in ancient times religion was supposed to carry this responsibility. But now in the community, religion generally seems a little bit old-fashioned, so people are losing interest in it and in deeper human values. However, I think these should be two separate things. If you have respect for or interest in religion, that is good. But even if you have no interest in religion, you should not forget the importance of these deeper human values.

There are various positive side-effects of enhancing one's feeling of compassion. One of them is that the greater the force of your compassion, the greater your resilience in confronting hardships and your ability to transform them into more positive conditions. One form of practice that seems to be quite effective is found in *A Guide to the Bodhisattva Way of Life*, a classic Buddhist text. In this practice you visualize your old self, the embodiment of self-centredness, selfishness and so on, and then visualize a group of people who represent the masses of other sentient beings. Then you adopt a third person's point of view as a neutral, unbiased observer and make a comparative assessment of the value, the interests and then the importance of these two groups. Also try to reflect upon the faults of being totally oblivious to the well-being of other sentient beings and so on, and what this old self has really achieved as a result of leading such a way of life. Then reflect on the other sentient beings and see how important their well-being is, the need to serve them and so forth, and see what you, as a third neutral observer, would conclude as to whose interests and well-being are more important. You would naturally begin to feel more inclined towards the countless others.

I also think that the greater the force of your altruistic attitude towards sentient beings, the more courageous you become. The greater your courage, the less you feel prone to discouragement and loss of hope. Therefore, compassion is also a source of inner strength. With increased inner strength it is possible to develop firm determination and with determination there is a greater chance of success, no matter what obstacles there may be. On the other hand, if you feel hesitation, fear and a lack of self-confidence, then often you will develop a pessimistic attitude. I consider that to be the real seed of failure. With a pessimistic attitude you cannot accomplish even something you could easily achieve. Whereas even if something is difficult to achieve, if you have an unshakeable determination there is eventually the possibility of achievement. Therefore, even in the conventional sense, compassion is very important for a successful future.

As I pointed out earlier, depending on the level of your wisdom, there are different levels of compassion, such as compassion which is motivated by genuine insight into the ultimate nature of reality, compassion which is motivated by the appreciation of the impermanent nature of existence and compassion which is motivated by awareness of the suffering of other sentient beings. The level of your wisdom, or the depth of your insight into the nature of reality, determines the level of compassion that you will experience. From the Buddhist viewpoint, compassion with wisdom is very essential. It is as if compassion is like a very honest person and wisdom is like a very able person – if you join these two, then the result is something very effective.

I see compassion, love and forgiveness as common ground for all different religions, irrespective of tradition or philosophy. Although there are fundamental differences between different religious ideas, such as the acceptance of an Almighty Creator, every religion teaches us the same message: be a warm-hearted person. All of them emphasize the importance of compassion and forgiveness. Now in ancient times when the various religions were based in different places and there was less communication between them, there was no need for pluralism among the various religious traditions. But today, the world has become much smaller, so communication between different religious faiths has become very strong. Under such circumstances, I think pluralism among religious believers is very essential. Once you see the value to humanity through the centuries of these different religions through unbiased, objective study then there is plenty of reason to accept or to respect all these different religions. After all, in humanity there are so many different mental dispositions, so simply one religion, no matter how profound, cannot satisfy all the variety of people.

For instance, now, in spite of such a diversity of religious traditions, the majority of people still remain unattracted by religion. Of the five billion people, I believe only around one billion are true religious believers. While many people say, 'My family background is Christian, Muslim or Buddhist, so I'm a Christian, Muslim or Buddhist,' true believers, in their daily lives and particularly when some difficult situation arises, realize that they are followers of a particular religion. For example, I mean those who say, 'I am Christian,' and during that moment remember God, pray to God and do not let out negative emotions. Of these true believers, I think there are perhaps less than one billion. The rest of humanity, four billion people, remain in the true sense non-believers. So one religion obviously cannot satisfy all of humanity. Under such circumstances, a variety of religions is actually necessary and useful, and therefore the only sensible thing is that all different religions work together and live harmoniously, helping one another. There have been positive developments recently and I have noticed closer relations forming between various religions.

So, having reflected upon the faults of a self-centred way of thinking and life, and also having reflected upon the positive consequences of being mindful of the well-being of other sentient beings and working for their benefit, and being convinced of this, then in Buddhist meditation there is a special training which is known as 'the practice of Giving and Taking'. This is especially designed to enhance your power of compassion and love towards other sentient beings. It basically involves visualizing taking upon yourself all the suffering, pain, negativity and undesirable experiences of other sentient beings. You imagine taking these upon yourself and then giving away or sharing with others your own positive qualities, such as your virtuous states of mind, your positive energy, your wealth, your happiness and so forth. Such a form of training, though it cannot actually result in a reduction of suffering by other sentient beings or a production of your own positive qualities, psychologically brings about a transformation in your mind so effectively that your feeling of love and compassion is much more enhanced.

Trying to implement this practice in your daily life is quite powerful and can be a very positive influence on your mind and on your health. If you feel that it seems worthwhile to practise, then irrespective of whether you are a believer or a non-believer, you should try to promote these basic human good qualities.

One thing you should remember is that these mental transformations take time and are not easy. I think some people from the West, where technology is so good, think that everything is automatic. You should not expect this spiritual transformation to take place within a short period; that is impossible. Keep it in your mind and make a constant effort, then after 1 year, 5 years, 10 years, 15 years, you will eventually find some change. I still sometimes find it very difficult to practise these things. However, I really do believe that these practices are extremely useful.

My favourite quotation from Shantideva's book is: 'So long as sentient beings remain, so long as space remains, I will remain in order to serve, or in order to make some small contribution for the benefit of others.'

five

Interdependence, Inter-connectedness and the Nature of Reality

In a discussion of interdependence, inter-connectedness and the nature of reality, the first question is: what is time? We cannot identify time as some sort of independent entity. Generally speaking, there are external matters and internal feelings or experiences. If we look at the external things, then generally there is the past, the present and the future. Yet if we look closely at 'the present', such as the year, the month, the day, the hour, the minute, the second, we cannot find it. Just one second before the present is the past; and one second after is the future. There is no present. If there is no present, then it is difficult to talk about the past and the future, since both depend on the present. So if we look at external matters, it would seem that the past is just in our memory and the future is just in our imagination, nothing more than a vision.

But if we look at our internal experiences or states of consciousness, the past is no longer there and the future has not yet come: there is only the present. So things become somewhat complicated when we think along these lines. This is the nature of interdependency, the Sanskrit word *pratityasamutpada*. This is a very useful idea and it is one of my favourite subjects.

There are two levels of interdependency: a conventional level and a deeper level. First I will deal with the conventional level. When we speak of the Buddhist principle of interdependence, which is often referred to as 'interdependent origination', we must bear in mind that there are many different levels of understanding of that principle. The more superficial level of understanding of the principle is the interdependent nature or relationship between cause and effect. The deeper level of understanding of the principle is much more pervasive and, in fact, encompasses the entire spectrum of reality. The principle of interdependent origination in relation to cause and effect states that nothing can come about without the corresponding causes and conditions; everything comes into being as a result of an aggregation of causes and conditions.

If we consider the law of nature, we see it is not created by karma or by Buddha, it is just nature. We consider that Buddhahood developed according to natural law. Therefore, our experiences of pain and suffering, pleasure and joy, depend entirely on their own causes and conditions. Because of this natural relationship between causes and their effects, the Buddhist principle states that the greater your undesirability of a particular experience, event or phenomenon, the greater effort you must put into preventing the aggregation of its causes and conditions, so that you can prevent the occurrence of that event. And the greater your desirability of a particular event, outcome or experience, the greater attention you must pay to ensure that these causes and conditions are accumulated so that you can enjoy the outcome.

I personally believe that the relationship between a cause and an effect is also a sort of natural law. I don't think that one could come up with a rational explanation as to why effects necessarily follow concordant causes and conditions. For instance, it is stated that afflictive emotional states like anger and hatred lead to undesirable consequences, and according to the Buddhist scriptures, one consequence of hatred and anger is ugliness. But there is not a full, rational account

as to *how* ugliness is a consequence of that particular afflictive emotion. Yet in a way one can understand it, because when you experience
very intense anger or hatred, even your facial expression changes and
you assume a very ugly face. Similarly, there are certain types of mental and cognitive emotional states which bring about almost instanta-
neous positive changes in your facial expression. These states bring
you presence of mind, calmness and serenity and such an emotional
state or thought could lead to a more desirable outcome. So one can
see a type of connection, but not a full rational explanation.

But one might feel that there are certain types of emotional states,
such as a very deep level of compassion, which are positive, yet, when
they occur within your mind, one might say that at that particular
instant there is no joy. For instance, a person may be fully under the
influence of compassion and therefore sharing the suffering of the
object of compassion. In that case, one could argue, from what I have
said earlier, that compassion cannot be said to be a positive cause. But
here I think one must understand that, while it is true that as a result
of compassion, because one is fully engaged in sharing the suffering of
the object of compassion, at that instant there is a certain degree of
pain, this is very different from a pain which is being suffered by
someone who is depressed, desperate and helpless and feels a loss of
hope. In the case of compassionate suffering, although the person is
undergoing a sort of pain, there is definitely a high degree of alertness,
and there is no loss of control because the person is, in a way, willing-
ly taking on the suffering of the other person. So on the surface these
emotional states might look as though they have a similar outcome,
but they are entirely different. In one case, the suffering is so over-
whelming that the person has lost control and has given way to it,
whereas in the case of compassion, the person is still in control of his
or her thought.

Now if you understand the importance of appreciating the interdependent relationship between cause and effect, then you will appreciate the teachings on the Four Noble Truths. The entire teaching on the Four Noble Truths is based on the principle of causality. When the causal principle that is implied in these teachings is elaborated, you read Buddha's doctrine of the Twelve Links of Dependent Origination. In that teaching he stated that, because there is a particular cause, its effects follow; because the cause was created, the effect came about; and because there was ignorance, it led to action or karma.

So here you find three statements: one is that because the cause exists, the effect follows; because the cause was created, the effect was produced; and because there was ignorance, it led to the action. Now the first statement indicates that, from an affirmative point of view, when causes are aggregated, effects will naturally follow. And what is also implied in that statement is that it is due to the mere aggregation of the causes and conditions that the effects come into being, and that, apart from the causal process, there is no external power or force such as a Creator and so forth which brings these things into being.

The second statement again points out another important characteristic of dependent origination, which is that the very cause which brings about the effects must itself have a cause. If the cause is an eternally existing, permanent absolute entity, then such an entity could not be itself an effect of something else. If that is the case, then it will not have the potential to produce an effect. Therefore, first of all there must be a cause; second, that very cause must itself have a cause.

And the third statement points out another important characteristic of the principle of dependent origination. It is that the effect must be commensurate with the cause – there must be a concordance between the two. Not just anything can produce anything; there must be a sort of special relationship between cause and effect. Buddha gave an example of ignorance leading to action. Here the implication is, 'Who commits that action?' It is a sentient being – and by committing an act motivated by an ignorant state of mind that being is in a way accumulating his or her own downfall. Since there is no living being that desires unhappiness or suffering, it is due to ignorance that the individual engages in an act which has the potential to produce undesirable consequences.

So we find that the entire Twelve Links of Dependent Origination fall into three classes of phenomena. First, there are afflictive emotions and thoughts; second, there is the karmic action and its imprints; and third, there is its effect: suffering. So the principal message is that suffering is something that we all do not desire, but it is a consequence or an effect of ignorance. Buddha did not state that suffering is an effect of consciousness, because if that was the case, then the process of liberation or the process of purification would necessarily involve putting an end to the very continuum of consciousness. One moral that we can draw from this teaching is that the sufferings which are rooted in afflictive and negative emotions and thoughts can be removed. This ignorant state of mind can be dispelled, because we can generate insight which perceives the nature of reality. So we see that the principle of dependent origination shows how all these 12 links in the chain of dependent origination which forms an individual's entry into the cycle of existence are inter-connected.

Now if we were to apply this inter-connectedness to our perception of reality as a whole, then we could generate a great insight from it. For instance, we would then be able to appreciate the interdependent nature of one's own and others' interests: how the interests and well-being of human beings is dependent upon the well-being of animals living on the same planet. Similarly, if we develop such an understanding of the nature of reality, we would also be able to appreciate the inter-connectedness between the well-being of human beings and the natural environment. We could also consider the present, the future and so forth. We would then be able to cultivate an outlook on reality which is very holistic and has very significant implications.

So in a few words, you can see that there are no independent causes of one's own happiness. It depends on many other factors. So the conclusion is that in order to have happier future for oneself, you have to take care of everything which relates to you. That is, I think, quite a useful view.

So far, I have spoken about the principle of dependent origination from the perspective of the first level of understanding. We can see in the Buddhist scriptures the importance of understanding this level of the dependent origination. In fact, one of the Mahayana texts known as *Compendium of Deeds*, in which Shantideva quotes heavily from Buddha's *sutras*, points out the need to first of all appreciate the inter-connectedness of all events and phenomena: how, due to the causal and conditional process, phenomena and events come into being; and how crucial it is to respect that conventional reality, because it is at that level that we can understand how certain types of experiences lead to certain types of undesirable consequences, how certain causes, certain types of aggregation of causes and conditions can lead to more desirable consequences, and so forth; how, in fact, certain events can directly affect our well-being and experience. Because there is that sort of relation, it is very crucial for practising Buddhists to first develop a deep understanding of the perspective of the first level. Then Buddha states that one should go beyond that understanding and question the ultimate nature of the things that relate to each other in this inter-connected way. This points towards the Buddha's teachings on Emptiness.

In the teachings on the Twelve Links of Dependent Origination, the Buddha states that, although sentient beings do not desire suffering and dissatisfaction, it is through ignorance that they accumulate karmic actions which then lead to undesirable consequences. Now the question then is: what exactly is the nature of that ignorance? What is the mechanism that really leads an individual to act against what he or she fundamentally desires? Here Buddha points to the role of afflictive emotions and thoughts, like anger, hatred, attachment and so forth, which blind the person's understanding of the nature of reality. If we were to examine the state of mind at the point when an individual experiences an intense emotion like hatred, anger or extreme attachment, we would find that, at that point, the person has a rather false notion of self: there is a kind of unquestioned assumption of an independently existing 'I' or subject or person which is perceived, not necessarily consciously, as a kind of a master. It is not totally independent from the body or mind, nor is it to be identified with the body or mind, but there is something there which is somehow identified as the core of the being, the self, and there is a strong sort of grasping at that kind of identity or being. Based on that, you have strong emotional experiences, like attachment towards loved ones, or strong anger or hatred towards someone whom you perceive as threatening, and so forth.

Similarly, if we were to examine how we really perceive our object of desire or object of anger, we would notice that there is a kind of assumption of an independently existing entity, something which is worthy of being desired or worthy of being hated. Aside from the subtle perspective of the doctrine of Emptiness, even in our day-to-day lives we often find a disparity between the way we perceive things and the way things really exist. If that was not true, then the very idea of being deceived would not make sense. We often find ourselves totally disillusioned because we had false perceptions of reality. Once our illusion is dispelled, we realize that we have been deceived. So we often see in our own daily life cases where the appearance of something does not tally with the reality of the situation.

Similarly, as I pointed out in my talk on subtle impermanence, even from the perspective of the transient nature of phenomena there is often a big disparity between the way in which we perceive things and the way things really are. For instance, when we meet someone we say, 'Oh, this is the very same person I've known for a long time.' Again, when you see an object, you think, 'Oh, this is the same object which I saw two days ago.' This is a very crude way of talking about reality. What is actually happening here is a kind of a conflation between an image or a concept of an entity and the actual reality of the moment. In reality, the object or entity that we are perceiving has already gone through a lot of stages. It is dynamic, it is transient, it is momentary, so the object that we are perceiving now is never the same as the one which we perceived a day ago or two days ago, but we have the impression that we are perceiving the very same one because what we are doing is conflating the concept of that object and the actual object. So we see again here a disparity between the way things appear to us and the way in which things really exist. Similarly, if we were to take the perspective of modern physics, then we would also find that there is a disparity between the common-sense view of reality and how scientists, from their point of view, would explain the nature of reality.

So what is clear from all this is the fact that there is some fault in our identification of an individual being as a self, as a person or as an individual. But the question is: to what extent is it false? We cannot accept that the self or 'I' does not exist at all, because if that is the case then a lot of our concerns, projects and actions would not make any sense. Because of the fact that there is a self, our concerns for attaining full liberation for the sake of other sentient beings, our concern for the well-being of other sentient beings, becomes very serious, because there is someone or something who would either suffer or benefit as a result of the stand we adopt or actions we engage in. So the question really is: to what extent is our notion of self, our sense of identity, our understanding of the being or individual, false or deceived, and to what extent is it correct? Making the demarcation between the correct view of the self and person and the false view of the self and person is extremely difficult. It is because of this difficulty – yet at the same time the importance of being able to make such a distinction – that there emerged in India various Buddhist philosophical schools. Some schools only accept 'identitylessness' of persons, but not of external events or phenomena; some schools accept the 'identitylessness' of not only persons but also of entire existence, and even within that school there are various subtleties.

The reason why so much importance is placed on making the distinction is because it is so crucial to our attempt to liberate ourselves from suffering and its causes. This in part answers one of the questions that arose in one of the previous talks, that, if Buddhism accepts the doctrine of 'no-self', what is it that takes rebirth?

We know that the doctrine of no-self or *anatman* is common to all the Buddhist schools of thought. The common doctrine of no-self is understood in terms of the denial of an independent and permanent self or soul. But what I will be presenting here is the understanding of Nagarjuna, as interpreted by the Indian pandit Chandrakirti. Nagarjuna, in his principal philosophical work, *The Fundamental Treatise on the Middle Way*, states that it is ignorance or misapprehension of the nature of reality which is at the root of our suffering. The manner in which one can attain liberation from suffering is by dispelling this ignorant state of mind, this misconceived notion of reality, by generating insight into the ultimate nature of reality. Nagarjuna identifies two types of ignorance: one is grasping at an inherent or intrinsic reality of one's own self or being; the other is grasping at an inherent and independent existence of external events and things. He goes on to state that this grasping at a 'self' or 'I' comes about as a result of grasping at our aggregates: our body, mind and mental functions. He further states that the fact that we have to dispel this ignorance from within our minds, that we have to see through the misconception of our misapprehension, is clear. But simply by distancing ourselves from that grasping, simply by thinking that it is false, simply by thinking that it is destructive and so on cannot ultimately help to free the individual from such forms of grasping. It is only by seeing through the illusion of that apprehension, it is only by generating an insight that would directly contradict the way in which, through that ignorance, we would normally perceive reality that we will be able to dispel that ignorance.

So how do we go about seeing through the illusion of this false notion of self? How do we generate the insight that would directly contradict that form of perception? Nagarjuna says that if a 'self', 'I' or person exists as we normally assume it to exist, if it exists as we falsely view it, then the more we look for it, the more we search for its essence, the referent behind our terms and labels, then the clearer it should become. But that is not the case. If we were to search for the self or person as we normally perceive it, then it disappears, it sort of disintegrates, and this is an indication that such a notion of self was an illusion from the start. Because of this point, one of Nagarjuna's students, Aryadeva, stated in his *Four Hundred Verses on the Middle Way* that it is our ignorant conception or consciousness which is the seed of *samsara* (cyclic existence) and that things and events are its objects of grasping and apprehension. And it is only by seeing through the illusion of such a conception that we will be able to put an end to the process of existence.

We find in Nagarjuna's own writings extensive reasoning to refute the validity of our notion of self and negate the existence of self or person as we falsely perceive it. He argues that if the self or person is identical with the body, then just as the body is momentary, transient, changing every day, the self or the person should also be subject to the same law. For instance, a human being's bodily continuity can cease and, if the self is identical with the body, then the continuum of the self will also cease at that point. On the other hand, if the self is totally independent of the body, then how can it make sense to say, when a person is physically ill, that the *person* is ill, and so forth? Therefore, apart from the interrelationships between various factors that form our being, there is no independent self.

Similarly, if we extend the same analysis to external reality, we find that, for example, every material object has directional parts, certain parts facing towards different directions. We know that so long as it is an entity it is composed of parts and that there is a kind of necessary relationship between the whole and its parts, so we find that apart from the interrelationship between the various parts and the idea of wholeness, there is no independent entity existing outside that interface. We can apply the same analysis to consciousness or mental phenomena. Here the only difference is that the characteristics of consciousness or mental phenomena are not material or physical. However, we can analyse this in terms of the various instants or moments that form a continuum.

Since we cannot find the essence behind the label, or since we cannot find the referent behind the term, does it mean that nothing exists? The question could also be raised: is that absence of phenomena the meaning of the doctrine of Emptiness? Nagarjuna anticipates the criticism from the realists' perspective which argues that if phenomena do not exist as we perceive them, if phenomena cannot be found when we search for their essence, then they do not exist.

Therefore, a person or self would not exist. And if a person does not exist, then there is no action or karma because the very idea of karma involves someone committing the act; and if there is no karma, then there cannot be suffering because there is no experiencer, then there is no cause. And if that is the case, there is no possibility of freedom from suffering because there is nothing from which to be freed. Furthermore, there is no path that would lead to that freedom. And if that is the case, there cannot be a spiritual community or *sangha* that would embark on the path towards that liberation. And if that is the case, then there is no possibility of a fully perfected being or Buddha. So the realists argue that if Nagarjuna's thesis is true, that the essence of things cannot be found, then nothing will exist and one will have to deny the existence of *samsara* and Nirvana and everything.

Nagarjuna says that such a criticism, that these consequences would follow from his thesis, indicates a lack of understanding of the subtle meaning of the doctrine of Emptiness, because the doctrine of Emptiness does not state or imply the non-existence of everything. Also the doctrine of Emptiness is not simply the thesis that things cannot be found when searched for their essence. The meaning of Emptiness is the interdependent nature of reality.

Nagarjuna goes on to say what he means by the claim that the true meaning of Emptiness emerges from an understanding of the principle of dependent origination. He states that because phenomena are dependent originations, because phenomena come about as a result of interdependent relationships between causes and conditions, they are empty. They are empty of inherent and independent status. An appreciation of that view is understanding of the true Middle Way. In other words, when we understand dependent origination, we see that not only the existence of phenomena, but also the identity of phenomena, depend upon other factors.

So dependent origination can dispel extremes of both absolutism and nihilism, because the idea of 'dependence' points towards a form of existence which lacks independent or absolute status, therefore it liberates the individual from extremes of absolutism. In addition, 'origination' frees the individual from falling to the extremes of nihilism, because origination points towards an understanding of existence, that things do exist.

I stated earlier that the unfindability of phenomena or entities when we search for their essence is not really a full meaning of Emptiness, but at the same time it indicates that phenomena lack intrinsic reality, they lack independent and inherent existence. What is meant by this is that their existence and their identity are derived from mere interaction of various factors. Buddhapalita, one of the disciples of Nagarjuna, states that because phenomena come about due to interaction of various factors, their very existence and identity are derived from other factors. Otherwise, if they had independent existence, if they possessed intrinsic reality, then there would be no need for them to be dependent on other factors. The very fact that they depend on other factors is an indication that they lack independent or absolute status.

So the full understanding of Emptiness can come about only when one appreciates the subtlety of this principle of dependent origination – if one concludes that the ultimate nature is that phenomena cannot be found if we were to search for their essence. Nagarjuna states that if the principle or doctrine of Emptiness is not valid, if phenomena are not devoid of independent and inherent existence and intrinsic reality, then they will be absolute; therefore there will be no room for the principle of dependent origination to operate and there will be no room for the interdependent principle to operate. If that is the case, it would not be possible for causal principles to operate and therefore the holistic perception of reality also becomes a false notion. And if that is so, then the whole idea of the Four Noble Truths will be invalid because there is no causal principle operating. Then you will be denying the entire teachings of the Buddha.

In fact, what Nagarjuna does is to reverse all the criticisms levelled against his thesis, by stating that in the realists' position all the teachings of the Buddha would have to be denied. He sums up his criticism by saying that any system of belief or practice which denies the doctrine of Emptiness can explain nothing coherently, whereas any system of belief or thought which accepts this principle of interdependent origination, this doctrine of Emptiness, can come up with a coherent account of reality.

So what we find here is a very interesting complementary relationship between the two levels of understanding of dependent origination I spoke of earlier. The perspective of the first level really accounts for much of our everyday existence or everyday world of experience, where causes and conditions interact and there is a causal principle operating. That perspective of dependent origination, according to Buddhism, is called the correct view at the worldly level. The greater your appreciation of that perspective, the closer you will be able to come to the deeper level of understanding of dependent origination, because your understanding of the causal mechanism at that level is used to arrive at an understanding of the empty nature of all phenomena. Similarly, once your insight into the empty nature of all phenomena becomes deep, then your conviction in the efficacy of causes and effects will be strengthened, so there will be a greater respect for the conventional reality and relative world. So there is a kind of interesting complementary relationship between the two perspectives.

As your insight into the ultimate nature of reality and Emptiness is deepened and enhanced, you will develop a perception of reality from which you will perceive phenomena and events as sort of illusory, illusion-like, and this mode of perceiving reality will permeate all your interactions with reality. Consequently, when you come across a situation in which you generate compassion, instead of becoming more detached from the object of compassion, your engagement will be deeper and fuller. This is because compassion is ultimately founded upon a valid mode of thought and you will have gained a deeper insight into the nature of reality. Conversely, when you confront situations which would normally give rise to afflictive, negative emotions and responses on your part, there will be a certain degree of detachment and you will not fall prey to the influences of those negative and afflictive emotions. This is because, underlying those afflictive emotions and thoughts, such as desire, hatred, anger and so forth, there is a mistaken notion of reality, which involves grasping at things as absolute, independent and unitary. When you generate insight into Emptiness, the grip of these emotions on your mind will be loosened.

At the beginning of my talk I gave an example of our concept of time: ordinarily we presume there is a kind of an independent existent or independent entity called 'time' present or past or future. But when we examine it at a deeper level, we find it is a mere convention. Other than the interface between the three tenses, the present, future and past, there is no such thing as an independently existing present moment, so we generate a sort of dynamic view of reality. Similarly, when I think of myself, although initially I might have an unquestioned assumption of there being an independent self, when I look closer I will find that, apart from the interface of various factors that constitute my being and various moments of the continuum that form my being, there is no such thing as an absolute independent entity. Since it is this mere conventional 'self', 'I' or person that goes towards the attainment of liberation or eventually transforms into Buddha, even Buddha is not absolute.

There is a similar case with the phenomenon mentioned earlier, the idea of Clear Light, which is the most subtle level of consciousness. Again, one should not conceive of it as some kind of independently existing entity. Apart from the continuum of consciousness which forms this phenomenon called Clear Light, we cannot speak of an independently existing absolute entity.

Likewise, we will find that many of our concepts indicate a very deep, very complex inter-connectedness. For instance, when we speak of ourselves as subjects, we can make sense of that notion only in relation to an object – the idea of a subject makes sense only in relation to an object. Similarly, the idea of action makes sense in relation to a being, an agent who commits the act. So if we were to analyse a lot of these concepts, we would find we cannot really separate the entity or the phenomenon from its context.

Again, if we go beyond the idea that things are mere designations or labels and ask whose conceptual thought creates the labels, whether it is the past conception or the future conception, whether it is the conception of a particular being or the collective conception, and so forth, we will not find an independent existence.

Even Emptiness itself, which is seen as the ultimate nature of reality, is not absolute, nor does it exist independently. We cannot conceive of Emptiness as independent of a basis of phenomena, because when we examine the nature of reality we find that it is empty of inherent existence. Then if we are to take that Emptiness itself as an object and look for its essence or its status of existence, again we will find that it is empty of inherent existence. Therefore Buddha taught the Emptiness of Emptiness. However, when we search for the true essence of a phenomenon or event, what we find is this Emptiness. But that does not mean that Emptiness itself is absolute, because

Emptiness as a concept or as an entity cannot withstand this analysis. If we were to take Emptiness itself as an object and then again examine it, we cannot find it. However in some scriptures we will find references to Emptiness as ultimate truth. Here one should understand what is the meaning of this term 'ultimate'. One should not mistake it in terms of Emptiness as being ultimately true, or it being absolute, but rather it is called 'ultimate truth' because it is an object of the insight that has penetrated into the nature of reality.

six

The Challenge for Humanity: An Interfaith Address

We have seen in this present age tremendous advances in the field of material development. As a result, there has been a marked improvement in the lives of human beings. Yet, at the same time, we are also aware that material development alone cannot answer all of humanity's dreams. Moreover, as material development reaches a higher and higher stage, we sometimes find that it brings with it certain complications, including more problems and challenges for us. Because of this fact, I think that all the major religious traditions of the world have the potential to contribute to the benefit and well-being of humanity, and also that they retain their relevance in the modern age.

However, since many of these major world religions evolved a long time ago in human history, I am quite sure that many aspects of their religious teachings and traditions reflect the needs and concerns of different times and cultures. Therefore, I think it is quite important to be able to make a distinction between what I call the 'core' and 'essence' of religious teachings and the cultural aspects of the particular tradition. What I would call the 'essence' or 'core' of religious traditions are the basic religious messages, such as the principles of love, compassion and so forth, which always retain their relevance and importance, irrespective of time and circumstances. But as time changes, the cultural context changes, and I think it is important for the followers of religious traditions to be able to make the necessary changes that would reflect the particular concerns of their time and culture.

I think the most important task of any religious practitioner is to examine oneself within one's own mind and try to transform one's body, speech and mind, and act according to the teachings and the principles of the religious tradition that one is following. This is very important. Conversely, if one's faith or practice of religion remains only at the intellectual level of knowledge, such as being familiar with certain doctrines without translating them into one's behaviour or conduct, then I think that is a grave mistake. In fact, if someone possesses certain intellectual knowledge of religious traditions or teachings, yet his or her consciousness and mental continuum remain totally uninfluenced by it, then this could be quite destructive. It could lead to a situation in which the person, because of having the knowledge of the religious beliefs, could use the religion for the purposes of exploitation and manipulation. So, I think, as practitioners, our first responsibility is to watch ourselves.

The situation of today's world is completely different from the past. In the past, human communities and societies remained more or less independent of one another. Under such circumstances, ideas of a single religion, a monolithic culture and so forth, made sense and had a place in the cultural context. But this situation has now completely changed as a result of various factors: easy access between various countries, an information revolution, easy transportation, and so forth. So human society can no longer function on that model.

Let us take as an example the city of London. London is a city which is multi-cultural and has multiple religions. Therefore, if we don't exercise caution and utilize our intelligence, there is a possibility of conflict based on divergent religious beliefs and cultures. So it is very important to have an outlook that takes into account the existence of multiple religions, the plurality of religions. The best way to meet this challenge is not just to study other religious traditions through reading books, but more importantly to meet with people from other religious traditions so that you can share experiences with them and learn from their experiences. Through personal contact you will be able to really appreciate the value of other religious traditions.

From a wider perspective, there are definitely strong grounds for appreciating pluralism in religion and culture, particularly in religion. It is a fact that among humanity there are many diverse mental dispositions, interests, needs and so on. Therefore, the greater the diversity of religious traditions that are available, the greater their capacity to meet the needs of different people.

In the history of humanity there have been very tragic events which came about because of religion. Even to this day, we see that conflicts arise in the name of religion and the human community is further divided. If we were to meet this challenge, then I am sure we would find that there are enough grounds on which we can build harmony between the various religions and develop a genuine respect towards each other.

Another important challenge facing humanity now is the issue of environmental protection. In fact, a number of prominent environmentalists have expressed their wish to see more active initiatives taken by the different religious traditions and especially by their leaders. I think this is a wish that is very valid. Personally, I feel that much of the environmental problem really stems from our insatiable desire, lack of contentment and greed. It is in the religious teachings that we find various instructions that enable us to keep a check on our desires and greed, and to positively transform our behaviour and conduct.

71

Therefore, I think religious traditions have not only a potential but also a great responsibility to make contributions in that direction.

Another thing that I consider very important, and which is a responsibility that religious traditions must take upon themselves, is the putting forward of a united front against war and conflict. I know that in human history there have been a few cases where, through war, freedom has been won and certain goals have been achieved. But I personally believe that war cannot ever lead to the ultimate solution of a problem. Therefore, I think it is important for all the religious traditions to take a united stand and voice their opposition to the very idea of war. But voicing one's opposition to war alone is not enough. We must do something to bring about an end to war and conflict, and one of the things that we have to seriously think about is the question of disarmament. I know that the motivating factor which triggers the need for weapons is human emotion – hatred and anger. But there is no way that we can completely eliminate anger and hatred from the minds of human beings. We can definitely reduce their force and alleviate them, but not completely eliminate them. That means that we have to make serious efforts to achieve disarmament.

Another challenge that we face is the question of population. I know that from the point of view of all religious traditions, life, human life in particular, is precious. From the viewpoint of individual human beings, the more humans there are the better it is, because then we have the opportunity for more human lives to come into being. However, if we look at this issue from a global perspective, then I think there is definitely a need for all religious traditions to give the population issue very serious thought, because the world's resources are limited. There is only a certain degree to which world resources can sustain human beings on this planet.

seven

Questions and Answers
on Various Problems of the Modern Age

Q:

On pollution and on the end of the universe

Your Holiness, what is your answer on how to stop pollution in the universe? Will there have to be an end of the universe and mankind as we know them in order to cleanse and begin again?

A:

Of course, from the Buddhist viewpoint, not just from that of common sense, there is a beginning and there is an end. That is logical; that is law; that is nature. So whatever we call the Big Bang or such things, there is a process of evolution or a process of beginning. So there must be an end. In any case, I think the end won't come for several million years.

Now, pollution. As you know I come from Tibet. When we were in Tibet, we had no idea about pollution. Things were very clean! In fact, when I first came across pollution and heard people say that I could not drink the water, it was a surprise to me. Eventually our knowledge widened.

Now it is really a very serious issue. It is not a question of one nation or two nations, but of the survival and health of all of humanity. If we have a clear conscience about this problem and behave accordingly, it seems there is a way to at least lessen this problem. For example, two or three years ago when I was in Stockholm beside the big river, some of my friends told me that 10 years previously there had been no fish in the river because the water was so polluted. Around the time of my visit some fish had begun to appear because of the control of pollution. So this shows that there is the possibility of improving things.

Killing and situations like Bosnia are immediately striking to our minds. Yet pollution and other environmental problems lack this kind of striking appearance. Gradually, month by month, year by year, things become worse and worse. By the time a problem becomes very obvious it may be too late. Therefore I think it is a very serious matter. I am quite encouraged that in many places people are clearly concerned, and even some political parties have been set up based on the ideology and policy of environmental protection. I think this is a very healthy development. So there is hope.

Q:
On human suffering

Your Holiness, in this modern world, we try to avoid suffering. This only seems to create more suffering in that one person's positive work can be someone else's suffering, for instance medicine, politics and so on. How do we judge? Shouldn't we just accept a certain amount of suffering and discomfort?

A:

I think that there are many levels of suffering. Generally speaking, it is definitely possible to reduce the level of suffering. I don't personally believe that conditions that are essential for one's well-being and happiness necessarily involve harming and affecting someone else's life in a negative way.

74

Here I would like to say something. I feel that television and newspapers usually report negative things. Killings, for example, or unfortunate events are immediately reported. In the meantime, millions of people are actually receiving help, or being nourished or looked after by human affection, such as millions of children, sick and old people. But usually in people's minds these good things are taken for granted. They are not seen as something to which we should pay special attention. Actually, this shows that the very nature of humanity is compassion or affection. We simply ignore all the work of affection because it seems natural. But we are surprised at things like bloodshed; it shocks our minds because our nature is not of that kind. As a result, many people get the impression that human nature is negative, aggressive and violent. I think that psychologically this is very bad, especially for young children who, through television, see negative human elements, but always for a short time. At that moment or for a short period, these things like killing or hitting can be a little bit exciting. But in the long-term, I think these violent things are very, very harmful to society. In fact, I recently had a meeting with Karl Popper, the philosopher. We have known each other since my first visit to this country in 1973. In our meeting we discussed violence on television and my view that too much violence is having a very negative impact on the minds of millions of children. He is, I think, of the same opinion. A proper way of education is the most important element in terms of hope for a better future.

Q:

On racism, bigotry and human folly

Your Holiness, racism, bigotry and human folly seem to be on the increase. To what negative factors do you ascribe this? What positive factors can combat this trend?

A:

I think they largely depend on education. I feel that the more correct information and the more awareness and contact you have, the better. Of course, you also have to adopt an open mind. After all, you are just one human being out of five billion and one individual's future depends very much on others. Part of the problem I see is a lack of awareness of other cultures and the existence of other communities, and also a lack of understanding of the nature or reality of modern existence. If it were possible to gain complete satisfaction and fulfilment by being totally independent within one's own culture and one's own community – to be totally independent and unrelated to other communities around the world – then perhaps one could argue that there were grounds for subscribing to these misconceptions like bigotry and racism. But this is not the case. The reality of the existence of other cultures and other communities cannot be ignored. Moreover, the nature of modern existence is such that the well-being, happiness and success of one's own community are very connected with the well-being and interests of other communities and other societies. In such a complex modern world there is no room for bigotry and racism.

Now according to my own experience, there is no doubt that Buddhism is the most suitable religion for me. But this does not mean that Buddhism is best for everyone. Each individual has a different mental disposition and therefore for some people a particular religion is more suitable or more effective than others. So if I respect each individual's right, then I must respect or accept the value of these different religions because they work for millions of other people.

When I was in Tibet I had little information, through books or from personal contact, about the nature and value of other traditions. Since I've become a refugee, I have had more opportunity to have closer contact with other traditions, mainly through individuals, and

I have gained a much deeper understanding of their value. As a result, my attitude now is that each one is a valid religion. Of course, even from the philosophical viewpoint, I still believe that Buddhist philosophy is more sophisticated, that it has more variety or is more vast, but all other religions still have tremendous benefits or great potential. So on both bases, I think my attitude towards other religions is greatly changed. Today, wherever I go and whenever I meet someone who follows a different religion, I deeply admire their practice and I very sincerely respect their tradition.

Q:

On bringing up children

What are the most important features in bringing up young children?

A:

I think you should ask a specialist. That would be better!

Q:

On money

How can one live well in a society based around the need to earn money?

A:

I think there is the possibility of balancing that with living well. For instance, even Tibetans need to earn money. Especially me at this moment with the exiled government – I think our deficit this year is over two million dollars! So I am very, very worried about that!

Q:

On birth control and the population explosion

Your Holiness, do you have any recommendations about the population explosion in the world?

A:

I think there is no doubt that birth control is necessary. Abortion is very, very sad. However, I think contraception is very necessary. Sometimes I jokingly tell people that it would be best if there were more nuns and monks. Isn't that the best non-violent method of population control?!

Q:

On religion in the modern world

Your Holiness, in this country there has been a move away from religion in recent years. At the same time, there has been an increased interest in various forms of self-development. Is religion still an appropriate path in the modern world?

A:

It is definitely relevant in the modern world. But perhaps I should clarify this. Many years have passed since various religious traditions started, so certain aspects are, I think, perhaps out of date. But this does not mean that religion as a whole is irrelevant in modern times. Therefore, it is important to look at the essence of the different religions, including Buddhism. Human beings, no matter whether today's or those of 100, 1,000, 4,000 or 5,000 years ago, are basically the same. Of course, a lot of the cultures and the ways of life have changed, but still we have the same kind of human being. So therefore, the basic human problems and suffering – such as death, old age, disease, fighting and all these things – are still there. I don't know what kind of shape humans will be in after 10,000 years or 100,000 years; nobody knows. But at least over the last few thousand years, they have, I think, kept basically the same nature.

So I think the various different religions actually deal with basic human suffering and problems. On that level, because human nature and suffering have remained the same, the religions are still very relevant. On the other hand, certain ceremonial aspects and so on have changed. In India, during the feudal system or the reign of kings, the way of practice was very much influenced by those circumstances. But that has changed and, I think, has to change further.

As far as Buddhism is concerned, it of course not only deals with this life but with other more mysterious aspects. Unless, just as modernization is taking place in our world, a similar type of modernization is taking place in other realms of existence, I think Buddhism will retain its relevance and appropriateness, not only to our modern world, because many of the fundamental problems of human existence still remain, but also because it addresses issues which are related to other mysterious forms of existence. I always believe that the modern change is just a surface change and that deep down we are the same. Last year at the border between Austria and Italy, they recovered an old body. If we were to suppose that the person was alive, I think we could still communicate with him. Yet the body is about 4,000 years old. Of course, that person would have a different culture and maybe a slightly different way of expression, but basically we could still communicate.

Q:

On retribution and the situation in Bosnia

You said that without hatred, retribution may be positive in order to prevent another from committing misdeeds. Would Your Holiness make any comment on the advisability of the United Nations authorizing air strikes against the Bosnian Serbs?

A:

Oh, that's really too complicated! The only thing we can do is simply share their misery and suffering. It's a very sad situation. Other than sharing their misery in our minds, there doesn't seem to be much we can really do. To me, all of these problems and chaotic situations in Bosnia, as well as in the former Soviet republics and in Africa, do not just come about suddenly. The causes of these developments run through decades. Therefore, we should learn from these events. In future, I think that if there is an area where there is the potential for this kind of crisis, the world community must pay full attention to it right from the beginning and take appropriate measures. I think this is very necessary.

Regarding human rights violations, now it is very encouraging that people all over the world have a new outlook regarding human rights issues. This is very healthy and good. But I consider human rights violations and similar sorts of problems also as symptoms. For instance, if there is some swelling or pimple on the surface of the skin, it is because something is wrong in the body. It is not sufficient to just treat the symptoms – you must look deeper and try to find the main cause. You should try to change the fundamental causes, so that the symptoms automatically disappear.

Similarly, I think that there is something wrong with our basic structure, especially in the field of international relations. I often tell my friends in the United States and here: 'You cherish democracy and freedom very much. Yet when you deal with foreign countries, nobody follows the principle of democracy, but rather you look to economic power or military force. Very often in international relations, people are more concerned with force or strength than with democratic principles.' I think I can go further: the highest international body, the United Nations itself, which was founded because of the situation just after World World II, has, for example, five nations with permanent seats in the Security Council, each with the power of veto. This is not democratic. Moreover, in Africa, where millions die from starvation, weapons are available but food is not. This area has real opportunities, but millions of dollars are spent on buying weapons! I think it's very sad.

So, as we have discussed, hatred is our enemy and weapons are also our enemy. Of course, when I was young I thought that weapons, air rifles, for example, were very beautiful. I loved to polish them! But the real purpose of these weapons is killing! Awful. We must do something about these beautiful but awful weapons.

And as for the military establishment... I think in the Western tradition, it is common for the son of the King or Queen to be sent to a military academy or into the navy. People feel proud of this. But I will tell you one small story. Last year, a German television team came to see me and one of the things they said was that, while Westerners are very, very afraid of death, Easterners do not seem afraid of death. I jokingly told them that the exact opposite was the case. You are so fond of military things. Not only do you yourselves build military forces, but you also sell arms. Arms and the military establishment are intended to kill. But in the East, even if one insect is killed there is a sense of repentance. For example, once, when I was in Tibet, a person was murdered and everyone was shocked. It was something really unbelievable. So it seems that Westerners are not afraid of death, while Easterners really fear death. I really feel that. So I think that mentally there's something wrong with the concept of war and the military establishment. One way or another, we must make every attempt to reduce the military forces. Anyway, with regard to the Bosnians and particularly your question about Bosnia, I have no clear answer – no idea.

Q:

On overcoming the negativity of the news and media

What suggestions can you offer to overcome social institutions, such as the news, entertainment and media, which seem constantly to promote negative attitudes and emotions – the opposite of what you advocate?

A:

That is true. I often express my concern at that. However, I think as we discussed, much depends on our own mental attitude. When we look at these negative things – killing, sex or that kind of thing – if we look at them from another angle, that is also useful. Sometimes you can use these scenes of violence, sex and so forth in a more positive way, so that, by being mindful of the effect and destructive nature of these various human emotions, you can use this particular viewing as a reminder of their destructive nature. While images of sex and violence may be somewhat exciting initially, if you look further you can see no benefit.

Of course, I have another opinion of the media, I think especially in the West. In a country like India, killing and murder is often shown on television, but the sexual things are more censored. But if you compare killing and sex, sex is much better! If we pretend that it is not a part of human life, that is also not good, is it?

Anyway, I think it is equally important to make a clear presentation to the human mind of the other, good, human qualities, and I think that this is lacking. We only show the negative side – killing, sex and all these things – but the other side, the human acts of compassion, are not shown.

Now, for example, about 10 days ago in Washington I visited the museum of the Holocaust. When I went there, after seeing all these things, I was reminded of both qualities of human beings. On the one side there was Nazi Germany's torture, killing and extermination of the Jewish people – horrible and very sad. It reminds me how bad or awful it is if human intelligence is guided or motivated by hatred. But at the same time, another side showed those people who sacrificed their own lives in order to protect Jewish people. So that also shows the human good quality, to risk even their own lives to save unfortunate people. In that way, I think it was quite balanced. If we let hatred guide us then we can be so cruel and so destructive. But on the other hand, if we promote good human qualities, then wonderful actions and marvellous things can happen. Likewise, the media should show both sides. That is what I always feel.

Q:

On genetic engineering

Scientists and doctors can now help people choose the sex of their baby. What does Your Holiness think about genetic engineering and what effect does it have on the unborn? Should the unborn have the choice, or the parents?

A:

I think it's very difficult to give a general answer to this. I think we have to study it case by case. Of course, in some cases such work may be positive; so that's difficult.

Q:

On the world's political leaders

Do you think that the world's political leaders use their 'brilliant brains' in a useful or pure way?

A:

Perhaps some, I think! I hope!

On Human Emotions

Q:

On transforming fear and despair

Is it possible for an ordinary person to transform his or her fear and despair? How can we do this?

A:

Oh, yes, it is very possible. For example, when I was young I was always afraid of dark rooms. As time went by, the fear went. Also, with regard to meeting people, the more your mind is closed, the greater the possibility of developing fear or feeling uncomfortable. The more open you are, the less uncomfortable you will feel. That is my experience. If I meet anyone, whether a great man, a beggar or just an ordinary person, to me there is no difference. The most important thing is to smile and to show a genuine human face. Different religions, different cultures, different languages, different races – these are not important. Educated or uneducated, rich or poor, there is no difference. When I open my heart and open my mind, I consider people just like old friends. This is very useful. On the basis of that kind of attitude, if the situation is something different then I have the freedom to act according to the circumstances. But at the beginning, from my side, I must create the ground. Then often there is a positive response from the human level. So I think fear is one thing to clear away.

Also, in the individual's mind there are many hopes. If one hope fails, it does not mean that all hopes fail. I have met some people who tend to feel completely overwhelmed and who become desperate when they are not able to fulfil one of their hopes. But I believe that the human mind is very complex. We have so many different types of hopes and fears that it is quite dangerous to invest everything on one particular hope, so that when that hope is not fulfilled we are totally overwhelmed. That is a bit too dangerous.

Q:

On dealing with attachment to material wealth and companions
You talked about dealing with attachment to our own body. What methods are effective in dealing with extreme attachment to material wealth and companions?

A:

For someone who accepts rebirth or any form of existence after death, there are various sorts of reflections that one can do, such as reflecting upon the ultimate futility of being too attached to one's companions or one's material wealth, or reflecting on the transitory or impermanent nature of these phenomena. One can reflect on how being extremely attached to these phenomena can increase one's afflictive emotions and lead to frustrations and so forth.

Now even if you are a non-believer or a genuine atheist, then if you look at the purpose of our lives, you will see that life is not simply meant for wealth or for your dearest ones. There are many other purposes. If you are a non-believer, I think you can still conduct certain types of contemplations as a means of reducing your extreme attachment towards material wealth and companions. For instance, you could think that material wealth and companions are definitely some of the various conditions for your happiness and sense of fulfilment, but that does not mean that these are the only conditions or means for your sense of fulfilment or satisfaction. Therefore, there is no point in being single-minded and investing all your energy in this, because it is not the only condition that you require for leading a happy and fulfilling life. In fact, similar types of contemplation can be found in classical Buddhist literature such as *Four Hundred Verses on the Middle Way*.

Q:

On true tolerance

Could Your Holiness speak a little more about inter-personal relationships in accordance with personal karma? How does one understand the difference between tolerance and stupidity?

A:

True tolerance is a stand or a response an individual adopts in relation to a particular incident, or towards another person or event, when the individual has the ability to act in a contrary manner. As a result of one's considerations, taking into account many factors and so on, the individual decides against taking negative action, and this is true tolerance. This is quite different from a situation in which an individual has no capacity whatsoever to take such a strong counter-measure. Then he or she is in a helpless position, so can't do otherwise. The difference between the two is in fact quite clearly pointed out in one of the Buddhist texts known as *Compendium of Deeds* by the Indian master Shantideva. So my tolerance towards the Chinese is actually quite open to question – is it really genuine tolerance or not?!

Q:

On overcoming fear

How may one overcome fear or fearfulness as a habitual state of mind, especially when there is no apparent cause?

A:

I think that the kind of outlook you have and the way you think makes a big difference. Often we find ourselves being hit by a sudden thought or feeling, such as fear, which, if we leave to itself, or, in other words, give in to without paying much attention, can begin to work in its own cause and begin to affect us. It is crucial that when such things arise one must apply one's faculty of reasoning so that one does not fall under the sway of these thoughts and feelings. Of course, if there is sufficient reason to fear, then fear is good! Fear creates preventive measures, so that's good. Yet if there is no basis for fear, then when you meditate analytically the fear will be reduced. That's the proper way.

Q:

On spontaneous compassion

Can compassion arise spontaneously after one has developed direct intuitive insight?

A:

I think it depends very much upon one's own spiritual orientation and the basic motivation. It is possible for certain practitioners who have developed familiarity with various principles of the Mahayana path, altruism and so forth. As the individual gains greater insight into the nature of reality, the greater the power of his or her compassion and altruism will be, because he or she will then see that sentient beings revolve in the cycle of existence due to ignorance of the nature of reality. Such practitioners, when they gain very deep insight into the nature of reality, will also realize the possibility of a way out from that state of suffering. Once you have that realization, then your compassion towards sentient beings will be greater because then you will realize their fate – although they can get out, they are still caught in the cycle.

But simply because one has gained a certain degree of insight into the nature of reality does not guarantee an automatic spontaneous experience of compassion. This is because one's insight into the nature of reality can be motivated by an altruistic wish to help other sentient beings or it can be induced by a motivation primarily concerned with one's own interest of attaining liberation from cyclic existence. So simply by generating insight into the nature of reality on its own cannot really lead to genuine compassion; you need some additional conditions.

Q:

On forgiveness

Can you speak about forgiveness? In my past I have done some wrong and questionable things, and feelings of guilt intrude on my peace of mind, although I work hard to repair the damage I have done. What actions can I take to aid my forgiveness of myself and others?

A:

If you are a practising Buddhist then it may be effective to engage in a form of purification practice which involves the application of what are known as the Four Powers, one of these being a sense of regret for the action committed. This already seems to be present. Another factor that is needed is a sense of resolve not to engage in such acts in the future. Complemented with these two factors, the actual purification practice could involve taking refuge in the Three Jewels and then engaging in certain religious practices, such as making prostrations and reciting mantras, meditating on love and compassion, or meditating on Emptiness, the ultimate nature of reality.

Q:

On the positive expression of anger

Are there examples of the positive expression of anger based on compassion and self-understanding?

A:

Yes, it is possible to have circumstances in which the basic motivation can be compassionate, but the immediate catalyst or motivating factor can be anger, which is a very strong force of mind.

Q:

On dissolving the pain of child abuse

If one is damaged or abused as a child, and in adult life the scars lead to depression and negative emotions, can we dissolve the pain through meditation? And is the process of psychotherapy complementary to the Way?

A:

I think it is best to use both techniques. It may differ according to the circumstances but, generally speaking, they are definitely complementary.

Q:

On staying in touch with your emotions

Your Holiness, how can I stay in touch with my emotions without being afraid? I often control my feelings so much that I am closed off and unable to love.

A:

When I talk about love and compassion, I make distinctions between the ordinary sense of love and what I mean by love. What I mean by love can arise on the basis of a clear recognition of the existence of the other person, and a genuine respect for the well-being and rights of others. However, love based on strong attachment towards one's close ones is, from the point of view of religious practice, something that has to be ultimately purified. A certain degree of detachment must be developed.

I think that perhaps at the beginning level you may find some kind of loneliness. Actually, that is one of the aims of the lives of monks and nuns. While in one way that sort of life may seem a bit colourless or unattractive, in another way it is more colourful. In reality, I think the one form of happiness has too much fluctuation, so I think in the long run the other type, although less dramatic, is something steady. In the long run I think that it is much more comfortable! So that is one consolation for monks and nuns!

Q:

On dealing with despair and depression

If someone feels in the depths of despair and, in a very deep depression, lies at night wanting to die, what is your advice to help that person become more stable and positive?

A:

It is very difficult if it is someone who has no background or practice. Then I really don't know what to advise. But if it is someone who has some experience of practice or some other religion, and if he or she has some experience of Buddhist practice, then it is helpful to think about Buddha Nature and about the potential of the human body and the

human brain. It is also helpful to read the stories of great practitioners of the past, whose lives illustrate the hardships that people have
gone through. For instance, in some cases these great masters were
people who had previously had almost no education or people who
were depressed and lacked facilities and so forth. But as a result of
their determination and confidence in their own potential, they were
eventually able to attain high realizations. One must also bear in mind
that being depressed and losing hope will never really help to correct
the situation.

Q:

On transforming the energy of anger and desire

Your Holiness, you spoke of the wrathful deities. Would you say some
more about transforming the energy of anger and desire through
Tantric practice. What is the key to such a transformation?

A:

Certain qualifications are necessary on the part of the individual who
is capable of transforming the energy of negative emotions like anger
and desire into the path. Such an individual must have a firm foundation in the realization of the path of wisdom and method. Based on
that, such a person must also have a certain degree of realization of the
deity yoga meditation: single-pointedness and also a firm identity and
appearance of the deity. Then there are certain forms of activities that
one can engage in which could enable the individual to transform
these energies, including the wrathful action. In order to take such
action, one needs some kind of wrathful motivation, such as a certain
anger which is entirely based on *karuna* or compassion. That also affects
swiftness. A satisfactory account would involve a long explanation.

On Buddhism

Q:

On right view and wisdom

Surely right view is the beginning of wisdom on the path? It is not just for religion.

A:

You are correct in saying that right view is not necessarily the special purview of religion. What I meant by stating that perverted or wrong views are one of the Ten Negative Actions from the religious point of view, is because in Buddhism, when the Ten Negative Actions are counted, the perverted or wrong views refer to disbelief in rebirth, disbelief in the possibility of attainment of Nirvana, and so on. These are definitely unique to Buddhist belief.

Q:

On meditation

How can meditation help bring about contentment?

A:

Generally speaking, when we use the term 'meditation' it is quite important to bear in mind that it has many different connotations. For example, meditations can be single-pointed, contemplative, absorptive, analytic and so forth. Especially in the context of the practice of cultivating contentment, the type of meditation that should be applied or engaged in is more analytical. You reflect upon the destructive consequences of a lack of contentment and the positive benefits of contentment and so forth. By reflecting upon these pros and cons, you can enhance your capacity for contentment. So if one's understanding of meditation is confined to a mere absorptive, single-pointed state of mind, without the application of the analytical faculty, I don't think that this type of meditation alone can lead to the development of contentment. This is because one of the basic Buddhist approaches in meditation is somehow to engage in a form of practice during the meditative session so that it can have a direct impact on one's post-meditative period, for example on our behaviour, our interaction with others and so on.

Q:
On karma

Karma is the law of cause and effect of our activity. What about the cause and effect of inactivity?

A:

Generally speaking, when one talks about the doctrine of karma, especially in relation to negative and positive karma, it is definitely linked with a form of action. But that does not mean that there are neutral actions or neutral karma, which can be seen as a karma of inactivity. For instance, if we are confronted with a situation in which someone is in need of help, suffering or in a desperate situation, and the circumstances are such that, by being actively engaged or involved in the situation, you can help or relieve the suffering, then if you remain inactive that can have a karmic consequences.

But a great deal depends upon one's attitude and motivation. So irrespective of whether the individual has the capacity to relieve a person from his or her suffering, if the person's attitude is such that he or she is totally indifferent to the other person's well-being and in a way abandons that person's well-being or need, that could definitely have negative karmic consequences. But this is quite different from a situation in which an individual does not necessarily wilfully disregard others' needs, but rather remains inactive out of a lack of confidence and a lack of courage. That can be seen as less negative.

Q:

On gaining confidence in our Buddha Nature
What is the best way to gain confidence in our Buddha Nature?

A:

Based on the concept of Emptiness, meaning the objective Clear Light, and also the concept of the subjective Clear Light, we try to develop a deeper understanding of Buddha Nature. It's not easy, but through investigation, I think both intellectually and through making connection with our daily feeling, there is a way to develop some kind of deeper experience or feeling of Buddha Nature.

Q:

On the nature of sentient beings and whether plants have Buddha Nature
Your Holiness, modern science cannot make a clear distinction between plants and simple forms of animal life. How does Buddhism decide who has mind and who doesn't? Would it be possible to believe plants participate in the cycles of existence and have Buddha Nature?

A:

At one of my meetings with scientists on the interface between modern science and Buddhism, the question was raised of how we determine whether a living thing is sentient or non-sentient. Eventually, all of us came to an agreement that the deciding factor is the capacity to move, mobility. Of course, from a Buddhist viewpoint there are other sentient beings who have no form, like those in the formless world. In addition, within the form realm where beings do manifest in physical form, Buddhist literature mentions sentient beings in the shape of plants, flowers and so forth. But as to the specific question of whether or not we can find out whether, for instance, the plant over here is sentient or not, I honestly don't know how to determine it. I think that on a conventional level people think, 'That's just a plant.' So we accept it as just a plant.

But still, one must take into account that in our perception of reality there are various levels of discrepancy between the way in which we perceive things and the way in which things and events really unfold. This may have some relation to a statement made in a Buddhist philosophical tenet known as *Madhyamika Prasangika*, which provisionally accepts the distinction between falsity and reality, illusion and reality, but ultimately does not accept such a distinction.

Q:

On conscious and subconscious beliefs

In attempting to view life in a positive light, how does Buddhism deal with the dichotomy between conscious and sub-conscious beliefs?

A:

Although I am not very clear about the meaning of the English term 'subconscious', according to Buddhism, when we talk about the means of overcoming various afflictive and negative cognitive and emotional states, we make a distinction between those which are conscious or manifest experiences and those which remain in the form of dispositions, predispositions or tendencies. Between the two, overcoming the conscious and manifest cognitive and emotional states is considered to be easier than overcoming the subtle tendencies and predispositions of mind. Therefore, in the Buddhist scripture, when presenting the path to Enlightenment, insight into the nature of Emptiness is seen as the counter-force for overcoming the obvious and manifest forms of these afflictive states. It is only through constant familiarity with the understanding of the nature of reality, through a long process of meditation, that one can eventually overcome tendencies and dispositions.

Buddhist literature mentions various stages in the process of overcoming afflictive and negative states. The first is to train oneself in such a way that at the initial stage the person has reached a level where, even though he or she might come across certain circumstances and conditions which normally would give rise to negative and afflictive responses, due to practice the person will not give rise to these negative states. This will then be followed by a more advanced state in which the person can actually directly counteract and prevent the arising of afflictive emotions. Finally, at a still more advanced stage, the person can actually remove the seed or potential that gives rise to such negative states. So, as you can see, the process of overcoming our negative and afflictive cognitive and emotional states is very complex. It is not just by generating an insight into the nature of reality that, in one instant, you can remove all the negativities from your mind.

To give you some idea of the complexity of the process, we can see that with regard to a particular issue our minds go through states which are quite different. For instance, one's position regarding a particular issue could, at the initial stage, be totally contrary to reality. As a result of trying to understand the exact reality of the situation, perhaps that single-minded misunderstanding can then be slowly questioned and turned into a wavering state, in which you think that maybe it is the case, maybe it is not. That wavering state of hesitation can then, through further analysis, turn into a state of presumption, tending towards the correct conclusion. When further reinforced and familiarized, that state of presumption can be turned into a state of true knowledge. At the initial stage, that true knowledge may only be an inference based on certain premises, and therefore conceptual. But through constant familiarity, eventually that inferential understanding can, according to Buddhism, culminate in a direct, intuitive understanding of the nature of reality. So you can see there is a kind of a progression. This in a way illustrates the complexity of the forces of overcoming our afflictive states. So according to Buddhism, a true state of cessation, in which the individual has totally overcome the effects of negative and afflictive emotions and cognitive states, is said to be a direct and intuitive insight.

Q:
On why Buddhism is described as a spiritual path
Your Holiness, why is Buddhism described as a spiritual path when everything revolves around the mind?

A:
Yes, it is true that some people describe Buddhism as a science of the mind rather than a religion. In the writings of one of the greatest Buddhist masters, Nagarjuna, it is mentioned that the approach of the Buddhist spiritual path requires the co-ordinated application of the faculty of faith and intelligence. Although I don't exactly know all the subtle connotations of the English term 'religion', I would personally think that Buddhism can be defined as a sort of combination of spiritual path and philosophical system. However, in Buddhism, greater emphasis is given to reason and intelligence than faith. Yet we do see roles for faith. For instance, Buddhism categorizes all phenomena into three classes: first, immediately obvious phenomena – those things which we can directly experience, or relate to and understand; second, certain types of phenomena which require inference through a logical process but which we can still infer from obvious premises; and third, phenomena which are called the 'obscure phenomena', which can be understood only by reliance upon the testimony of a

third person and, in the context of Buddhism, the testimony of the Buddha. By reliance on Buddha's word we accept their existence.

But even then the testimony of Buddha is not taken simply on blind faith just because he is the Buddha, but rather because Buddha's word has been proven reliable in the context of phenomena and topics which are amenable to logical reason and understanding. By inferring that Buddha has been proven reliable in these matters, one can then conclude that Buddha's word can also be taken as valid on issues or topics which are not so immediately obvious to us. So there is a kind of a role for faith there, but still we can see that it ultimately depends on reason and intelligence or one's understanding. So Buddhism can be described as a combination of a philosophical system and a spiritual path, or, rather, it can be seen as a combination of a mental science and a spiritual path.

One of the reasons why I say that in Buddhist methodology, especially in Mahayana Buddhist methodology, greater emphasis is placed on reason and understanding, is because we find in Mahayana Buddhism a distinction between two different categories of Buddha's words. Certain types of Buddhist scriptures can be taken as literal and definitive, and certain types cannot be taken at their face value, are not accepted literally and require further interpretation. How do we determine whether a certain type of scripture is literal and definitive or whether it requires further interpretation to determine the meaning below the surface? That can be done only by reliance on a form of reasoning. So ultimately understanding and investigation are the judge. This spirit is very clearly illustrated in Buddha's oft-quoted statement: '*Bhikshus* and wise men do not accept my words just because they are the words of the Buddha, simply out of reverence for me, but just as a goldsmith would test the gold through various procedures and then finally make a judgement, similarly accept the validity of my statements only after you have subjected them to analysis and investigation.'

So in a way Buddha gave us liberty to carry out further investigation of his own words. It seems that among humanity, one group of people describe themselves as radical materialists and another group base themselves solely on faith, without much investigation. Here are two worlds or two camps. Buddhism belongs to neither one. From one side Buddhism is a science of the mind, so that one side rejects it, saying it is not a religion. From the other side, Buddhism is too spiritual; it involves meditation and things like that, so that the other side rejects it. Thus Buddhism remains between the two. Perhaps that's one advantage: we can work as a bridge to bring these two extremes together. Sometimes I feel that in the future there may be an important role for Buddhism in bringing both sides together.

Q:

On celibacy

Is celibacy required for Enlightenment?

A:

I think generally not. Yet you may ask why Buddha himself eventually became a monk. I think, from the viewpoint of the *Viniya Sutra*, the main purpose of celibacy is to try to reduce desire or attachment.

From the viewpoint of Tantrayana, particularly the Highest Yoga Tantrayana, the energy, 'drops' or special bliss is the source of energy to dissolve the grosser level of consciousness or the grosser level of energy. Through experience of that special bliss, there is the possibility that the grosser level will eventually dissolve. So the drops are the key factor for the bliss.

In Tibetan Buddhism, especially if you look at the iconography of deities with their consorts, you can see a lot of very explicit sexual symbolism which often gives the wrong impression. Actually, in this case the sex organ is utilized, but the energy movement which is taking place is, in the end, fully controlled. The energy should never be let out. This energy must be controlled and eventually returned to other parts of the body. What is required for a Tantric practitioner is to develop the capacity to utilize one's faculties of bliss and the blissful experiences which are specifically generated due to the flow of regenerative fluids within one's energy channels. It is crucial to have the ability to protect oneself from the fault of emission. It is not just a purely ordinary sexual act. And here we can see there is a kind of special connection with celibacy. Especially in the practice of the Kalachakra Tantra, this precept of protecting oneself from the emission of energy is considered to be very important. The Kalachakra literature mentions three types of blissful experience: one is the blissful experience induced by the flow of energy; one is the immutable blissful experience; and one is the mutable blissful experience. To me, when Buddha took the celibacy vow, at that level he did not explain all the reasons behind that rule or that discipline. The complete explanation comes when we know the Tantrayana system. Perhaps that answers your question. So, I think the answer is both 'Yes' and 'No'!

Q:

On women and celibacy

The answer you gave about the need for celibacy and use of bliss and non-emission was from a man's point of view. Why is a woman's part in these practices never mentioned? What does a woman need to do with her energy to gain Enlightenment through bliss?

A:

It is the same technique and the same principle. According to some of my Indian friends, practitioners of Hindu Tantrayana also realize the practice of *kundalini* and *chandralini*. My information is that the female also has some kind of energy, drops. So it is the same method.

Q:

On the form of our rebirth

Who or what determines what we come back as?

A:

According to Buddhism, it is karma, one's own action, that really determines rebirth. Also the state of mind at the point of death has a crucial role. Those who have some familiarity with Buddhism may already know that there is a principal doctrine taught by the Buddha known as the 'Twelve Links in the Chain of Independent Origination'. The second link in the chain is karma. However, the presence of karma alone is not sufficient to lead to a rebirth, therefore circumstantial conditioning factors such as afflictive emotions and cognitive events are necessary. These are the eighth and the ninth links, which are attachment and grasping. So when the karmic imprint is activated by the force of the eighth and the ninth links, attachment and grasping respectively, then the karmic imprint becomes mature, which is the tenth link, known as the link of becoming. So the nature of one's rebirth basically depends upon the karmic imprints and potential of the individual being, not only accumulated during the present life but also during his or her previous lifetimes. Also, within the karmic potentials there might be some that are more forceful or powerful and some which are less powerful. *Abhidharma Kosha*, a Buddhist text, mentions that among the 'karmic potentials' or 'karmic seeds' that one might possess within one's mental continuum, it is the most forceful one that would determine the nature of rebirth. And if the individual has many equally strong forces of karmic imprints, then it is the karmic action which is closest to the present life that would come into fruition. And if there are still many karmic imprints of a similar nature, then it is the karmic action which the individual is most familiar with that would lead to fruition and determine the next rebirth. As I mentioned yesterday, one of the determining factors or conditions is the state of mind at the point of death.

Q:

On using the dream state

Could you say more about using the dream state?

A:

It is only in the highest Yoga Tantra, Tantric Buddhism, that we find meditative techniques that can be applied during the dream state. There are two main purposes for such types of meditation using dream-state consciousness. As I pointed out yesterday, it is during the dream state that we have an opportunity to rehearse or become familiar with the processes of dying, because there is a kind of an analogous process of dissolution experienced during the dream state. In a way, meditators rehearse by utilizing the dream state so that they can become familiar with the dissolution processes and train themselves to be able to recognize the various signs that are associated with various levels of dissolution.

But the principal purpose of dream meditation is to train oneself in such a way that, even during the dream state, the individual can actually experience what is known as the Clear Light, the most subtle level of consciousness, thus enabling him- or herself to actually experience dissolution of various elements during the dream state. And for that you require the capacity to recognize dreams as dream states. There are two principal methods for doing that. One is through Prana Yoga, which is the practice of the energy channels and which is quite an advanced method and is difficult for beginners. The other method is not so much through the practice of Prana Yoga, but rather through developing a sort of a determination or mental force – developing a strong will to identify or recognize dream states as dream states. It also has many connections with the type of diet you adopt, your behaviour and so on.

Q:

On the recognition of women in Tibetan Buddhism
Why has there not been any recognition in Tibetan Buddhism of women on the level of lamas or gurus?

A:
Actually there are some very high reincarnate institutions, like Samdring Dorje Phagmo, that traditionally are women lamas of a very high position. The current Samdring Dorje Phagmo Lama is the four-teenth incarnation. This demonstrates that this institution seems to be as old as that of the Karmapa, which is considered the first reincarnate institution in Tibet.

So there are a few reincarnated female lamas. Of course, the major-ity, both now and in the past, are male. One must admit that in the past, the position of women may have been neglected or not given much thought. Part of the reason for this negligence of the rights and position of women within Tibetan Buddhism is because in the past people simply did not give much thought to it. We more or less took the status quo for granted. For example, I recently had a meeting in

Dharamsala with some Western Buddhist teachers during which a point was made that in the ordination ceremony there are instructions about how to determine the seniority of ordination and that the custom seemed to really reflect a bias. At the meeting I promised that within six months I would organize a big conference, at least among our Tibetan scholars and *bhikshus*, to discuss these things.

Overall, I think that in the Buddhist system, especially in the *Viniya Sutra*, men and women both have the right to the highest ordination, the *bhikshu* and the *bhikshuni*. Yet it is also a fact that the *bhikshu* remains higher and *bhikshuni* lower. Then in Bodhisattvayana, everyone is believed to have the same Buddha Nature. In addition, the capability of achieving the level of Bodhicitta and of practising the six *paramitas* is exactly the same.

Now, regarding the exact Buddhist stand on the issues of gender, discrimination, women's rights and the position of women in Buddhism, as I pointed out earlier, as far as the presence of Buddha Nature is concerned, there is no difference. Nor is there any difference in terms of the potential that an individual has for generating the highest altruistic aspiration to attain Buddhahood or insight into the ultimate nature of reality and so forth.

But one must accept that there is certain Buddhist literature which does reflect a kind of discrimination. For instance, in one of the texts, *Abhidharma Kosha*, in which certain characteristics or features of an advanced level of Bodhisattva are mentioned, one of the characteristics seems to be that the person who is on an advanced path towards Enlightenment is in the form of a male practitioner. So it does seem to reflect some bias. But if we were to look at the issue from what I see as the highest stand-point of Buddhism, which, according to our understanding, is the position of the Highest Yoga Tantra, I would say there is no discrimination based on gender, because in the practice of

Highest Yoga Tantra you first of all require initiation into the practice, and initiation of Tantra is not complete without the full, equal participation of both female and male practitioners. For instance, both male and female can receive empowerment. Also, in the deity yoga mandala, the full participation of both male and female deities is necessary. And where Tantra is concerned, there are in fact specific precepts for Tantric practitioners which say that if you belittle or disparage a woman it constitutes an infraction of a Tantric precept. Similarly, on the path, full experience of the Tantric path towards Enlightenment can come about only if there is a complementary practice between both male and female practitioners. For example, if the practitioner is male then he requires assistance, a stimulus, from the opposite sex; and similarly, if the practitioner is a female, she requires assistance, a stimulating factor, from the male practitioner. This touches upon the topics we discussed about the generation of blissful states of mind; but this is completely different from ordinary sex. Similarly, both female and male practitioners can become fully Enlightened in their form as males and females. So from the stand-point of Highest Yoga Tantra, I would say there is no difference or discrimination based on gender.

I think it's very important for women to try to appropriate all their rights. Among the Tibetan refugee community in India, I have for many years been advocating for the female side, the nuns' side. They must have the interest or courage to study as the monks do. While at times in Tibet, almost none of the nunneries were places of serious study, there are legends of a different past in which there were nunneries which were important centres of philosophical learning and debate, so much so that there were several cases of debates between monks and nuns and the monks lost! So you see, for more than 20 years in India I have been continually making an effort for the female side, and they also must take the full initiative – that's important.

Q:

On determinism

Some people and teachers say that when you perform an act or make a decision, it is not really you making that decision, and what is meant to happen will happen regardless of the fact that you thought you made the decision or had an effect on some activity or situation. If this is so, how do we create karma, if it is not really us making the decision?

A:

I think that is the wrong conception. If this sort of fatalistic account of our actions and existence is true, then the very idea of the possibility of liberation or Enlightenment simply would not make any sense. Because the idea of Enlightenment entails that we completely change our karma and that salvation or Buddhahood is achieved. It is an entirely new initiative, which never happened in the past. That is exactly what is meant by practising, embarking on a spiritual path. I mentioned earlier that sometimes people, including Tibetans, use karma as a sort of excuse. I think that's wrong.

Q:

On meditation without purification of motivation

About great harm when meditation is practised without purification of motivation: I have met people who have achieved some power of the mind and use this power with a selfish, even cruel, motivation, with their minds crystallized or blocked and their hearts literally hard or impure. Is there any method of de-crystallization of energies fastened together in a wrong way?

A:

What is important is to have a very balanced approach in one's meditation. In fact, because of this significance in Buddhist teachings we often talk of 'comprehensive path'. For instance, if someone were to concentrate solely on generating insight into Emptiness without paying much attention to the development of the more compassionate aspects of the mind, then that can in fact result in a lower path. Similarly, if one puts all one's concentration on the development of the compassionate factors of the path, without paying any attention to the wisdom and intelligence aspect, then one's altruistic aspiration and attitude can never be really fully enhanced because they will be lacking the complementary factor. So generally one could say there are two distinct approaches in an individual's practice of the Buddhist path. One is engaging in a Buddhist practice of the path based on the development of understanding of the entire framework of the Buddhist path and how most of the key elements fit within a certain framework. However, there could be another approach which could be seen as more individualistic, in which an individual may not have a full understanding of the entire general framework of the Buddhist path, but simply follows single-pointedly an instruction given by an experienced master. Then the master is really extremely important and must be really qualified. That is then some exceptional case, without extensive study.

Q:

On blind faith

What do you feel about blind faith in order to reach Enlightenment?

A:

I don't think one can get far!

Q:

On compassion and the dependence of others

Your Holiness, in trying to be a compassionate human being, how responsible should we feel? What should you do if you find someone emotionally dependent on your compassion? Is it compassionate to hurt someone if you think it is the best in the long run?

A:

I think you should keep in mind compassion with wisdom. It is very important to utilize one's faculty of intelligence to judge the long-term and short-term consequences of one's actions.

Q:

On the significance of the actions of one individual

I can understand how my own mind and actions can affect my own causes and conditions. Can they also affect world conditions like hunger, poverty and other great sufferings of beings everywhere? How?

A:

Sometimes we feel that one individual's action is very insignificant. Then we think, of course, that effects should come from channelling or from a unifying movement. But the movement of the society, community or group of people means joining individuals. Society means a collection of individuals, so the initiative must come from individuals. Unless each individual develops a sense of responsibility, the whole community cannot move. So therefore it is very essential that we should not feel that individual effort is meaningless – you should not feel that way. We should make an effort.

Questions and Answers

Q:

*On whether beginners should proceed slowly or
quickly in learning Buddhism*

Would you advise Western beginners on the Buddhist path to proceed slowly and cover less ground or to try to learn as much as possible and proceed faster?

A:

Again, it depends on the individual case. I think in some cases extensive study is more suitable or useful. But it is important to keep one thing in mind: you should realize that spiritual development takes time; it doesn't happen just overnight. Perhaps some lama may say, 'Oh if you follow my teaching you will gain some spiritual experience within one week or two weeks.' I think that's nonsense.

Q:

On Clear Light mind

Your Holiness speaks of an innate Clear Light mind. This appears to come from Dzogchen discourse. In fact, the concept of an innate mind is the object of refutation by the *Madhyamika Prasangika* dialectic. Some Gelugpa hierarchies have even considered the Dzogchen tenet to be heretical and non-Buddhist. Yet Your Holiness has developed a way to integrate these two seemingly contradictory views of ultimate nature. Could you explain how Dzogchen is compatible with Lama Tsong Kapa?

A:

First, I think you have made a mistake. Perhaps there might be some confusion here between two sorts of apparently quite similar but actually very different concepts. On the one hand there is innate Clear

Light mind, and on the other, what I have referred to as 'innate grasping at an enduring self'. These are two different things. Innate grasping at an enduring sense of self is in fact still at the conceptual level where the thought processes are still active. That's when the innate grasping of self still operates, whereas innate Clear Light mind becomes manifest only at the most subtle level. But by that time much of the conceptual thought processes have already ceased their functioning, so these are two different things.

But as to the actual nature of Clear Light mind, whether it is still conceptual or non-conceptual, there are divergent opinions. Another difference is that Clear Light mind is being generated inside to perceive the nature of reality. In fact, this is one of the most powerful attitudes for overcoming the grasping at an enduring notion of self. It is stated that when the objective Clear Light, which is the Emptiness conjoined or assimilated with the subjective experience of Clear Light, which is the one innate mind that is being referred to here, the most powerful awareness to counteract the force of grasping is realized. I think when we talk about Gelugpa's position or stand-point we have to identify that more with Lama Tsong Kapa, the founder of the Gelugpa tradition, and to his two main disciples. We find that in one of the writings of Khnanpuje, one of the two foremost disciples of Lama Tsong Kapa, a question was raised as to the authenticity and efficacy of the Dzogchen view of ultimate nature. Khnanpuje says that so far as the actual view of the ultimate nature of Dzogchen tenets is concerned, it is an authentic view, something that can be definitely applied in one's practice of Highest Yoga Tantra. But the reason why there has been criticism of the Dzogchen view is because some of the Dzogchen practitioners around that time seemed to demonstrate a certain degree of laxity towards ethical principles.

But one thing we have to bear in mind here is the usage of the term 'view' – the right view – the view of Emptiness. In the Madhyamika literature, when the view of Emptiness is mentioned, the reference is often more towards the object of Emptiness, the nature of reality as it is, whereas when this term 'view' is used in the Dzogchen terminology and Mahamudra literature, then the reference is more to the subjective experience rather than the Emptiness. This distinction is quite important and it must be appreciated, because if we compare the view of Emptiness between Sutra and Tantra from the point of view of the understanding of Emptiness itself there is no difference. But a difference does emerge from the subjective point of view in that the Tantric subjective experience of Emptiness is said to be more profound.

Q:

Your Holiness, if you could have three wishes, what would they be?

A:

That is top secret!

On Various Aspects of Death and Dying

Q:

On accidental or sudden death

Your Holiness, what may happen to one who dies in an accident, such as in a car accident or by murder and so on?

A:

Under such circumstances, the individual may find himself or herself in a state of extreme anxiety or shock, but generally speaking, the state of mind in such situations can be described as neutral – neither virtuous nor non-virtuous. One thing that I've noticed among the findings of researchers who have done investigations into the phenomena of rebirth based on the testimony of children who claim to recollect their past lives is that in many of the cases, the manner in which the previous life's death was met was quite sudden, like accidents and so forth. So I feel there might be something here which needs a lot of research. From a Buddhist viewpoint, as far as I know there is no particular explanation.

In India about 10 years ago I met two girls, one from the Punjab and one from Uttar Pradesh. In both cases, the girls had had sudden deaths in their previous lives. One of these small girls had a truly remarkable memory of her past life. As a result, even her parents in her previous life accepted this new young girl as their own daughter, so in fact she has four parents! I began to wonder whether there might be some connection. First, both were female in this life and in their previous lives, and second, both had died suddenly. Perhaps the woman's mind is clearer! I don't know! If that is the case, I think in future there may be more reincarnation among females!

Q:

On differences between a peaceful and a sudden or violent death
Your Holiness, please could you speak about any differences which may exist between a peaceful death and a sudden and violent death?

A:

Of course, from the practitioner's viewpoint the natural death is better. There is more time to think and to practise. Also, according to Tantrayana, there are indications when different elements absorb. If the body is relatively strong, these indications of the dissolution of the different elements are clearer, so the practice becomes easier. If, however, the dying person has had a long illness and has become very weak physically, then the indications may not be very clear. There are certain types of meditative techniques in Buddhism known as 'transference of consciousness', to which a meditator is recommended to apply only as a last resort, and which enable the individual to go through the dissolution processes consciously and with awareness. Prior to that there are various types of indication that could help the meditator ascertain the certainty of his or her death. When these indications keep repeating and there is no possibility of reversal of the eventuality, then the meditators can turn to the last-resort practices like transference of consciousness. But the process of natural death is much better.

Q:
On preparation for death and the comatose state
If someone has prepared well for death, does it matter if he or she is in a coma up to and at the point of death? Will such a person still have the clarity of consciousness you mentioned as important?

A:
Although it's very difficult to judge the difference between the two states, if I were to guess perhaps I could say that, even though an individual might be a trained meditator, if he or she remained in a state of coma then perhaps it might affect his or her ability to discern the various indications of the dissolution processes. Although at the time of the actual dissolution process, the discernment is not really the same as the gross conceptual state of ascertainment that we normally experience, still the conscious will to discern the dissolution signs does have an impact and an effect on one's ability to remain aware at the time of death. Ideally it would be nice if we could do some experiments on this phenomenon and see, for instance, whether the ability of a trained meditator suffering from physical illness and in a coma to remain in a Clear Light state was affected or not.

Actually, some years ago in Dharamsala a team of scientists came and carried out some experiments. They wanted to investigate the process of death, so they brought one simple machine. But who can say who will die when? And who will have an experience? Nobody can predict this! It is a problem. Since that time there have been more than a few cases in which, after death, the bodies have not decayed. I think in some cases it has been for up to a week and in other cases for longer periods. But when those instances took place, nobody could conduct an experiment. Yet when the scientists were visiting with their equipment, nobody died! That is one difficult job!

Q:

On being HIV positive and dealing with anger and death
Your Holiness, as someone who is HIV positive, I find that anger at my state stops me from working at looking at death with equanimity. What can help with this anger?

A:

That is a problem. To a large extent society's attitude is also not very healthy because there is a tendency to marginalize those with HIV. In addition, the people themselves are completely discouraged or have a very low state of mental strength. But if individuals have some sort of practice, like Buddhist practice, then of course they can see that this life is just one life and that the end of this life is not the end forever. Also, every event and experience of this life is, of course, due to our own action or karma, not necessarily in previous lives but also due to action within this lifetime. According to the law of causality, these unfortunate things are due to one's own previous actions. So that is also a consolation I think.

I have met some Tibetan practitioners who have told me of their experiences. Some patients suffering from terminal illness ask for their doctor's honest opinion as to whether their illness can be cured or not, and if their illness is terminal, how long do they have to live. Once these patients know that they have only a certain amount of time left, they say to me that it comes as a kind of relief, because then they can re-orient their lives so that they can get their priorities right. So I think a great deal depends on one's own practice. Other than that, I don't know – it's difficult.

Q:

On euthanasia

In cases of agonizing terminal illness or injury, would you condone an assistance to death or mercy killing?

A:

That is also very complicated. Again, much depends on the individual case. From the Buddhist practitioner's viewpoint, since these situations are due to past karma or one's own action, sooner or later one has to go through these painful experiences. In such cases, it is better to have pain with this human body, because at least there are nurses and doctors who can take care of you. If it happens in some other form of life, there is no such facility and then the same experience is really hopeless. So this is one way of looking at it.

On the other hand, if one is in a state of coma and there is no hope of recovery, and if one remains like this for a long period, it is very expensive, and the expense may create some other problems. Such a complicated situation may perhaps be an exceptional case, but this is very difficult to say or to generalize. I think one has to decide based on individual cases.

Perhaps one could see some parallels between the practice of mercy killing and the Buddhist practice of transference of consciousness, the difference being that in one case the transference of consciousness is practised upon oneself. There is also a difference in objectives. In the case of mercy killing the motive may be to relieve the individual from extreme pain and agony, whereas in the case of transference of consciousness, it is more to do with granting the individual the opportunity to utilize the occasion of death before his or her bodily elements reach such a stage where the indications of the dissolution process may not remain vivid. So there might be some similarities.

Q:

On dealing with pain at death

Has Your Holiness any advice on dealing with pain at the time of dying?

A:

For someone who is a practitioner, at such moments it is possible for the effects of one's practices to have positive results, but otherwise it is very difficult to say what can actually be of benefit at that time. That's why, from a young age, these methods or practices are useful, no matter whether the individual is fully qualified or not. One should familiarize oneself with them, so that when the time comes one can deal with these things without much effort. That is the proper way. If one believes that, until the serious situation happens, one does not need to take the practice seriously, then when things become really desperate, it is very difficult and too late.

A great deal depends on how familiar you are with certain types of practice. For instance, if you are quite well trained in various techniques, such as meditation on love and compassion, meditation on the 'identitylessness' of phenomena, and meditation on the impermanent nature of existence, and you have practised giving and taking – giving one's prosperity, happiness and so forth to others and taking upon oneself others' suffering, pain, etc. – then at the time of death you could either reflect upon each training of mind in turn, or you could pay special attention to a particular form of practice. And because of your former familiarity, you will be able to place the main part of your mind or consciousness on the practice to such an extent that it would make even physical pain or suffering less obvious, and pain would affect you less. Similarly, if your power of concentration is great, then you can in fact focus on the very point where you have pain and then meditate on special practices, like visualizing white light or subtle drops or certain objects or mantras or whatever on that specific point, and that would help reduce the physical pain. But if you lack such familiarity and training, then it's very difficult to judge what could be the best method to overcome pain at that moment.

Q:
On karma and prolonging life unnecessarily
Following what you have said about karma, if one is in a healing profession, what are the karmic responsibilities regarding interfering or preventing the death process from taking place, or prolonging life unnecessarily?

A:
Generally speaking, I don't see any contradiction between a health professional helping a patient to remain alive and the karmic responsibilities involved in it, because when we talk of death, from the Buddhist perspective, it is experienced as a result of many factors, not just karma alone. There would be a death experience as a result of karmic consequence, for instance, if the karmic potentials have been exhausted; or sometimes the death can be an untimely one, as a

consequence of circumstantial conditions; and in some cases, death can be experienced, not because of the exhaustion of full fruition of a karma, but because of an exhaustion of the meritorious potential. Similarly there are different types of illness: karmically caused illness versus illness for which the primary condition or cause is more external or more internal.

The karmically caused death refers to situations in which, in spite of all possible means of preventing it, death cannot be avoided. Generally speaking, that type of experience of death is considered karmically caused. Moreover, in the case of sudden death, where the conditions can be seen as more external, even then karma plays a role. For instance, in the case of prolonging someone's life, the very fact that it is possible to prolong it or that there are conditions for prolonging it, is in a way a consequence of karma.

Actually I have noticed, even among Tibetans, that sometimes people as individual human beings do not take the initiative and that they use karma as a sort of excuse. I think that this is absolutely wrong. Who creates karma? We ourselves, by our actions, create karma. For example, if I want to write something down, that very action creates new circumstances and causes some other result or event. It is cause and effect, cause and effect. To think that karma is some sort of independent energy is wrong! Our daily lives, our good food or good work, our relaxation – everything is through action. It is all action and result, action and result. Whose action? Our action! Sometimes I think that there is some kind of misunderstanding when we talk about karma.

Even if you have already accumulated some negative karma, you still have the opportunity to change or to overwhelm that negative karma by virtuous karma. So everything depends on our own action. That is important. As a Buddhist practitioner, it is very essential to know that. A true practising Buddhist will have conviction in the existence of Buddha Nature, which allows the possibility of attaining the fully Enlightened state, a state of perfection. If that is the case, then why can't the individual have the conviction that he or she can overcome various problems?

The theory or doctrine of karma involves a lot of complex issues, so it is impossible to merely generalize and say that everything is a product or consequence of karma. For instance, in the case of my present physical body, like my hand here, the fact that this part of my body is so intimately linked with my experience and my physical sensations of pain and pleasure is very evident. But if we were to trace the physical cause of this particular part of my body, we could trace it back to the beginning of time. It is a material phenomenon, or a product of a material phenomenon, which can be traced to an earlier state and an earlier state and so on, until we reach a state in which it is a pure atom or particle. According to Buddhist literature that particle is technically called a 'space particle'. So as a result of this process of evolution throughout billions of years, that minute particle has now fully evolved into this animate physical body which can act as a basis for the arising of sensations of pain and pleasure. So the fact that this body is my body may be seen as a result of karma, but the fact that this body is a consequence of the beginningless continuum of material particles cannot be seen as a product of karma; it is simply the law of nature. Material objects come from material sources.

Similarly, when we look at the difference between mind and body, we find that there are certain central features that distinguish the two. For instance, material phenomena have certain features that make them physical or material. They are obstructive, whereas mental phenomena have the nature of clarity, luminosity and knowing, but they are not physical; they are not obstructive. The fact that these two exist in such a contrasting or different way is simply a law of nature. We cannot say it is because of karma that they are two different things.

Mahayana Buddhist literature takes this complexity of reality into account and shows that there are different ways of approaching the nature of reality. Buddhist literature mentions four principles for understanding the nature of reality. One is the principle of logical inference, which can be applied on the basis of our understanding of the ultimate nature of reality, but which can be applied only if there is a certain causal connection or inter-relatedness between phenomena – the fact that something can give rise to something else or that when certain things aggregate they can result in a certain outcome. On the basis of that principle of dependence we can apply logical inference.

And then that principle of dependence is possible because, for instance, matter and mind, or matter and consciousness, enjoy a different status of existence or different characteristics. The fact that there are such differences is simply a law of nature and in the Mahayana Buddhist literature, that is known as the principle of Natural Law. Taking into account this complexity of the nature of reality, we have to approach an understanding of the nature of reality by many different avenues of reasoning. So determining the influence of karma is difficult. Although we can say that a lot of the things that we experience are products or consequences of karma, determining how far the karmic influence reaches and how much is a consequence of the mechanisms of the natural law is open to dispute. It is something that we should examine and understand, but it is very difficult.

Q:
On facing the death of friends

Your Holiness, you face your own death with ease and peacefulness. How about the death of your friends?

A:

I don't know. With regard to my own feelings, yes, sometimes I am very sad – I was particularly sad when my immediate elder brother, Lobsang Samten, passed away. I think among my sisters and brothers, he was the brother whom I spent the most time with when I was young, especially when I came from my birthplace to Lhasa. I think the journey took over two months. Do you know about palanquins? There was a small one and we two brothers sat in it. We were very playful and when we both went on one side of the palanquin, the whole thing tilted. Then the person who was in charge of it would immediately shout from the outside, 'Don't do that! Don't do that!' For him, the best thing was if we two brothers quarrelled; then we had a clear demarcation: I sat here, he sat there. Then the thing was more balanced! The person who looked after that palanquin wasn't very happy I think! So when my brother passed away, I really felt extraordinarily sad. But then, that is a fact. Since his death I have occasionally wondered, 'Oh, where is his rebirth? In this world or in some other place? If it's in this world, where?' Sometimes this feeling comes.

Q:

On the intermediate state of mind between death and rebirth
You described an intermediate state of mind between death and rebirth. Is this linked to any kind of physical or biochemical processes, or is it independent of physical processes?

A:

The fact that such an intermediate state has no connection or link with the present body is quite obvious according to the texts. It is described in the texts that such a being has a body which is by nature subtle energy, not a corporeal body, but it is also described as possessing

a type of colour and shape. An analogy used in describing the body of
the intermediate state being is that of a dream body. It is said that
some advanced meditators can, during the dream state, actually
assume a dream body, and that body is said to be very similar to the
body of an intermediate state being. A dream body can naturally be
experienced by some individuals, whereas some individuals can deliberately attain it.

You have asked about subtle energy, or some aspect of subtle mind.
Yet you see colour and sometimes shape. It is a complicated matter,
but it seems to me that there are the external five elements and the
internal five elements, and within the internal there are the grosser
level of the five elements and the most subtle elements. In the most
subtle base, there is Clear Light. Clear Light is one aspect; another
aspect is the subtle energy. In that energy there is some kind of seed of
the five elements. So when we discuss the Clear Light as a foundation
of all existence, I think there is some link with external, solid things
and Clear Light. There is a mention of a particular energy force in the
Tibetan Buddhist literature technically called the Energy with Five
Radiances, and I think some connection can be seen between the
macroscopic world of our everyday experience and the microscopic
world of subtle energy. The link which is provided between the two
can be understood by understanding the nature of this particular energy force which is mentioned in the texts. What is so crucial here in
furthering our understanding of this connection is to see whether
there is any significant relation between this particular energy force
and what I have described as the space particles. I myself do not have
as yet a fully developed idea.

Q:

On knowledge of death and the Tibetan Book of the Dead
Is the knowledge of the processes of death to be formed by reading the
Tibetan Book of the Dead?

A:

Yes, it is helpful. As for the process of death, particularly the various
features and characteristics of the intermediate state, we sometimes
find sort of divergent presentations in the Abhidharma literature and
the Tantric literature. So perhaps it is best to try to have a broader
understanding by reading more texts. However, most of the visualiza-
tions and the visions that are described in the *Tibetan Book of the
Dead* may be considered more specific to a particular practitioner of
deities known as the mandala of the wrathful and the peaceful deities
as mentioned in that text.

On the Situation in Tibet

Q:

On dealing with Tibet and a large non-Buddhist Chinese population
If you returned to an independent Tibet, would it be difficult to rec-
oncile the Buddhist principles of compassion with the reality of gov-
erning a state with a large Chinese non-Buddhist population?

A:

I have already noticed during the last few decades so much degeneration in Tibetan culture and the Tibetan way of life. Besides our
Chinese brothers and sisters, even among Tibetans it seems there is
some danger. Take, for example, some young Tibetans who have
escaped from Tibet in the last few years – although their sense of being
a Tibetan is strong and very good, certain aspects of their behaviour

make me grow more anxious. They immediately fight or use force and, in recent months, there have been two murder cases involving young Tibetans who have escaped from Tibet. Every other aspect of their motivation is excellent, but there is so much degeneration in their humbleness or honesty and compassionate attitude. So even in India among our own people, these kind of things are happening. Due to these recent events I have really developed genuine concern. What is really happening inside Tibet, my country?

But then that's reality, so we have to face it. Still, I believe that when we have freedom – freedom of speech, freedom of thought, freedom of movement – we can minimize these things. Although in the future, when we have freedom, I will no longer be the head of the Tibetan government. That is my final decision. In fact, we have made an official document that says that as soon as I reach a free Tibet, we will form an interim government and I will hand over all my legitimate authority to that government. Within two years, that government will organize the Tibetan People's Assembly. Then it will decide the Tibetan constitution. So that is something that is already decided.

Q:
On His Holiness' future role in Tibet

Your Holiness, you said earlier that the changing attitudes of some of your Tibetans makes you anxious. So I wondered why you have decided to give up your historic authority in Tibet when it would seem that young people need spiritual rather than political guidance.

A:

The fact that I will no longer be the head of the Tibetan government does not mean that I will give up my moral responsibility or commitment. Of course, being a Tibetan, particularly since I am so trusted, it is my obligation to serve, to help humanity in general and particularly those people who very much trust me, till my last breath. In fact, the one reason why I do not want to carry the responsibility of government is that, after all, I am already 57, so I consider that I have about another 20 years of active life; then I will be too old. In any case, within the exile community in India we are already stepping up the democratic system. Within the next 20 years, democracy must be established. Otherwise at the initial stage there may be turbulence, disturbances or complications. All these complications should occur within my lifetime and then in the future things may go more smoothly.

Also, if I continue to carry the responsibility, although I think many Tibetans might appreciate this, indirectly it would become an obstacle for the healthy development of democracy. Therefore, I decided I must be out. There is another advantage: if I remain as the head of the government and a problem develops between the Tibetan central government and local people or an administration, then my presence could lead to further complications. If I remain as a third person, then I can work to solve such serious matters.

Also, personally, I do not want to be involved in ceremonial things. I don't like them and it's an extra burden. I would like to have more freedom to move here and there without any protocol. It is much easier and better, isn't it? For these reasons I have made my decision. But this does not mean that I will give up my responsibility or my commitment.

Q:

On using violence to free Tibet

Your Holiness, wouldn't sacrificing your beliefs in using violence to free Tibet be a worthwhile action, as this would result in the alleviation of suffering of the Tibetan people?

A:

No, I don't think so. In that situation, more violence would happen. That may lead to more publicity and that may help. But after all, the most important thing is that China and Tibet have to live side by side, whether we like it or not. Therefore, in order to live harmoniously, in a friendly way, and peacefully in the future, the national struggle through non-violence is very essential.

Another important matter is that the ultimate agreement or solution must be found by the Chinese and Tibetans themselves. For that we need support from the Chinese side, I mean from the Chinese people's side; that is very essential. In the past, our stand was the genuine non-violent method; this already creates more Chinese support, not only from the outside but inside China also. There are more supporters amongst the Chinese for our cause. As time goes on, more and more Chinese are expressing their deep appreciation and their sympathy. Sometimes they still find it difficult to support the independence of Tibet, but they appreciate our way of struggle. I consider this to be very precious. If Tibetans take up arms, then I think we will immediately lose this kind of support.

Q:

On support for Tibet

What would your Holiness like the members of the audience to do to help the Tibetan cause?

A:

Although I am very, very encouraged to receive great support from many different places like the United States and here in Britain, we still need more active support. You see, the Tibetan issue is not only a human rights issue, it also involves environmental problems and the issue of decolonization. The most important issue at present is the question of Chinese population transfer. At this moment we need more support to stop this demographic change. This is very, very crucial. Whatever way you can show support, we appreciate it very much.

The Four Noble Truths

Fundamentals of the Buddhist Teachings
His Holiness the XIV Dalai Lama

Translated by Geshe Thupten Jinpa
Edited by Dominique Side

Contents

Introduction   133

1 Introducing the Four Noble Truths   152
2 The Truth of Suffering   157
3 The Truth of the Origin of Suffering   175
4 The Truth of Cessation   189
5 The Truth of the Path   201

Appendix: Compassion, the Basis for
Human Happiness   210
Glossary   222
Recommended Reading   227

Introduction

The Four Noble Truths are the very foundation of the Buddhist teaching and that is why they are so important. In fact, if you don't understand the Four Noble Truths, and if you have not experienced the truth of this teaching personally, it is impossible to practise Buddha Dharma. Therefore I am always very happy to have the opportunity to explain them.

Generally speaking, I believe that all the major world religions have the potential to serve humanity and develop good human beings. By 'good' or 'nice', I don't mean that people look good; I mean that they have a good and more compassionate heart. This is why I always say that it is better to follow one's own traditional religion, because by changing religion you may eventually find emotional or intellectual difficulties. For example, here in England the traditional religious culture is Christian, so it may be better for you to follow that.

However, for those of you who really feel that your traditional religion is not effective for you, and for those who are radical atheists, then the Buddhist way of explaining things may hold some attraction. Maybe in this case it is all right to follow Buddhism – generally, I think it is better to have some kind of religious training than none at all. If you really feel attracted to the Buddhist approach, and the Buddhist way of training the mind, it is very important to reflect carefully, and only when you feel it is really suitable for you is it right to adopt Buddhism as your personal religion.

There is another very important point here. Human nature is such that sometimes, in order to justify our adoption of a new religion, we may criticize our previous religion, or our country's traditional religion, and claim it is inadequate. This should not happen. Firstly, although your previous religion may not be effective for you, that does not mean it will completely fail to be of value to millions of other people. Since we should respect all human beings, we must also respect those who are following different religious paths. Furthermore, your previous religion – like all religions – does have the potential to help certain types of people. It is clear that for some people the Christian approach is more effective than the Buddhist one. It depends on the individual's mental disposition. We must therefore appreciate that potential in each religion, and respect all those who follow them.

The second reason is that we are now becoming aware of the many religious traditions of the world, and people are trying to promote genuine harmony between them. One example of this is the interfaith gathering in Assisi in 1986[1] on religions and the environment. I think there are now many interfaith circles and the idea of religious pluralism is taking root. This is a very encouraging sign. At such a time, when people are promoting genuine religious understanding in many areas, a single individual's criticism can be very harmful. So on these grounds, we should maintain a spirit of respect for other religions.

I wanted to begin with these points, because when I actually explain the Four Noble Truths, I have to argue the Buddhist way is the best! Also, if you were to ask me what the best religion is for me personally, my answer would be Buddhism, without any hesitation. But that does not mean that Buddhism is best for everyone – certainly not. Therefore, during the course of my explanation, when I say that I feel that the Buddhist way is best, you should not misunderstand me.

I would like to further emphasize that when I say that all religions have great potential, I am not just being polite or diplomatic. Whether we like it or not, the entire human race cannot be Buddhist, that is quite clear. Similarly, the whole of humanity cannot be Christian, or Muslim, either. Even in India during the Buddha's time, the entire population did not turn to Buddhism. This is just a fact. Furthermore, I have not just read books about other religions but I have met genuine practitioners from other traditions. We have talked about deep, spiritual experiences, in particular the experience of loving kindness. I have noticed a genuine and very forceful loving kindness in their minds. My conclusion therefore is that these various religions have the potential to develop a good heart.

Whether or not we like the philosophy of other religions isn't really the point. For a non-Buddhist, the idea of nirvana and a next life seems nonsensical. Similarly, to Buddhists the idea of a Creator God sometimes sounds like nonsense. But these things don't matter; we can drop them. The point is that through these different traditions, a very negative person can be transformed into a good person. That is the purpose of religion – and that is the actual result. This alone is a sufficient reason to respect other religions.

There is one last point. As you may know, Buddha taught in different ways, and Buddhism has a variety of philosophical systems such as Vaibhashika, Sautrantika, Chittamatra and Madhyamaka. Each one of these schools quotes the word of the Buddha from the Sutras. If the Buddha taught in these different ways, it would seem that he himself was not very sure about how things really are! But this is not actually the case; the Buddha knew the different mental dispositions of his followers. The main purpose of teaching religion is to help people, not to become famous, so he taught what was suitable according to the disposition of his listeners. So even Buddha Shakyamuni very much respected the views and rights of individuals. A teaching may be very profound but if it does not suit a particular person, what is the use of explaining it? In this sense, the Dharma is like medicine. The main value of medicine is that it cures illness; it is not just a question of price. For example, one medicine may be very precious and expensive, but if it is not appropriate for the patient, then it is of no use.

Since there are different types of people in the world, we need different types of religion. Let me give you one example of this. At the beginning of the 70s, an Indian engineer showed a keen interest in Buddhism and eventually became a monk. He was very sincere and a very nice person. Then one day I explained to him the Buddhist theory of *anatman*, the theory of no-self or no-soul,[2] and he was so frightened by it he was shaking all over. If there really was no permanent soul, then he felt there was something very fundamental missing. He was literally shivering all over. I found it very difficult to explain the meaning of anatman to him; it took months. Eventually his shivering grew less and less. So for such a person, it is better to practise a teaching that is based on atman, or a belief in the soul.

If we are aware of all these points, then it is very easy to respect and appreciate the value of traditions other than our own.

Basic Principles of Buddhism

Whenever I introduce the Buddhist teachings, I make a point of presenting them in terms of two basic principles. The first of these is the interdependent nature of reality.[3] All Buddhist philosophy rests on an understanding of this basic truth. The second principle is that of non-violence, which is the action taken by a Buddhist practitioner who has the view of the interdependent nature of reality. Non-violence essentially means that we should do our best to help others and, if this is not possible, should at the very least refrain from harming them. Before I explain the Four Noble Truths in detail, I propose to outline both these principles by way of background.

Taking Refuge and Generating Bodhichitta

First, I will introduce these principles in traditional Buddhist terms. Technically, we become a Buddhist when we decide to take Refuge in the Three Jewels, and when we generate *bodhichitta*, which is known as compassion, the altruistic mind, or our good heart. The Three Jewels of Buddhism are the Buddha; the Dharma, his teaching; and the Sangha or community of practitioners. It is very clear that the idea of helping others lies at the heart of both Refuge and Bodhichitta. The practice of Generating Bodhichitta explicitly entails committing oneself to activities which are primarily aimed at helping others; while the practice of Taking Refuge lays the foundation for the practitioner to lead his or her life in an ethically disciplined way, avoiding actions that are harmful to others and respecting the laws of karma.

Unless we have a good foundational experience of the practice of Taking Refuge in the Three Jewels, we will not be able to have a high level of realization of bodhichitta. It is for this reason that the distinction between a practising Buddhist and a non-Buddhist is made on the basis of whether or not an individual has taken Refuge in the Three Jewels.

However, when we talk about Taking Refuge in the Three Jewels, we should not imagine that it simply involves a ceremony in which we formally take Refuge from a master, or that merely by virtue of participating in such a ceremony we have become a Buddhist. There is a formal Refuge ceremony in Buddhism, but the ceremony is not the point. The point is that as a result of your own reflection, even without a master, you become fully convinced of the validity of the Buddha, Dharma and Sangha as the true ultimate objects of refuge, and that is when you actually become a Buddhist. You entrust your spiritual wellbeing to the Three Jewels, and this is what is really meant by Taking Refuge. On the other hand, if there is any doubt or apprehension in your mind about the validity of Buddha, Dharma and Sangha as being the ultimate objects of refuge, even though you may have taken part in a Refuge ceremony, that very suspicion or doubt prevents you from being a practising Buddhist, at least for the time being.

It is therefore important to understand what these objects of refuge are.

When we speak about Buddha in this context, we should not confine our understanding of the word to the historical person who came to India and taught a certain spiritual way of life. Rather, our understanding of buddhahood[4] should be based on levels of consciousness, or levels of spiritual realization. We should understand that buddhahood is a spiritual state of being. This is why the Buddhist scriptures can speak about past buddhas, buddhas of the present and buddhas of the future.

Now the next question is: how does a buddha come into being? How does a person become fully enlightened? When we reflect on buddhahood, we are bound to ask ourselves whether or not it is possible for an individual to attain such a state, to become a fully enlightened being, a buddha. Here we find that the key lies in understanding the nature of Dharma. If the Dharma exists, then the Sangha will certainly exist – the Sangha are those who have engaged in the path of the Dharma, and who have realized and actualized its truth. If there are Sangha members who have reached spiritual states where they have overcome at least the gross levels of negativity and afflictive emotions, then we can envision the possibility of attaining a freedom from negativity and afflictive emotions which is total. That state is what we call buddhahood.

In the present context, I think we must make a distinction between the use of 'Dharma' as a generic term and its use in the specific framework of the Refuge. Generically, it refers to the scriptural Dharma – the Buddha's teaching and the spiritual realizations based on the practice of that teaching. In relation to the Refuge it has two aspects: one is the path that leads to the cessation of suffering and afflictive emotions, and the other is cessation[5] itself. It is only by understanding true cessation and the path leading to cessation that we can have some idea of what the state of liberation is.

Dependent origination

In the Sutras, Buddha stated several times that whoever perceives the interdependent nature of reality sees the Dharma; and whoever sees the Dharma sees the Buddha.[6] It is my belief that if we approach this statement from the perspective of Nagarjuna's teachings of the Madhyamaka School, we can arrive at the most comprehensive understanding of its implications. If you were to accuse me of having a bias in favour of Nagarjuna, I would certainly accept that criticism! So following Nagarjuna, we find there are three levels of meaning here.

Firstly, the understanding of the principle of interdependent origination (*pratityasamutpada*) that is common to all Buddhist schools explains it in terms of causal dependence. 'Pratit' means 'to depend on', and 'samutpada' refers to 'origination'. This principle means that all conditioned things and events in the universe come into being only as a result of the interaction of various causes and conditions. This is significant because it precludes two possibilities. One is the possibility that things can arise from nowhere, with no causes and conditions, and the second is that things can arise on account of a transcendent designer or creator. Both these possibilities are negated.

Secondly, we can understand the principle of dependent origination in terms of parts and whole. All material objects can be understood in terms of how the parts compose the whole, and how the very idea of 'whole' and 'wholeness' depends upon the existence of parts. Such dependence clearly exists in the physical world. Similarly, non-physical entities, like consciousness, can be considered in terms of their temporal sequences: the idea of their unity or wholeness is based upon the successive sequences that compose a continuum. So when we consider the universe in these terms, not only do we see each conditioned thing as dependently originated, we also understand that the entire phenomenal world arises according to the principle of dependent origination.

There is a third dimension to the meaning of dependent origination, which is that all things and events – everything, in fact – arise solely as a result of the mere coming together of the many factors which make them up. When you analyse things by mentally breaking them down into their constitutive parts, you come to the understanding that it is simply in dependence upon other factors that anything comes into being. Therefore there is nothing that has any independent or intrinsic identity of its own. Whatever identity we give things is contingent on the interaction between our perception and reality itself. However, this is not to say that things do not exist. Buddhism is not nihilistic. Things do exist, but they do not have an independent, autonomous reality.

Let us now refer back to the statement by the Buddha, when he said that seeing dependent origination leads to seeing the Dharma. There are three different meanings to this concept of Dharma which correspond to the three different levels of meaning of dependent origination which we have just described.

Firstly, we can relate Dharma to the first level of meaning of dependent origination, which is causal dependence. By developing a deep understanding of the interdependent nature of reality in terms of causal dependence, we are able to appreciate the workings of what we call 'karma', that is, the karmic law of cause and effect which governs human actions. This law explains how experiences of pain and suffering arise as a result of negative actions, thoughts and behaviour, and how desirable experiences such as happiness and joy arise as a result of the causes and conditions which correspond to that result – positive actions, emotions and thoughts.

Developing a deep understanding of dependent origination in terms of causal dependence gives you a fundamental insight into the nature of reality. When you realize that everything we perceive and experience arises as a result of the interaction and coming together of causes and conditions, your whole view changes. Your perspective on your own inner experiences and the world at large shifts as you begin to see everything in terms of this causal principle. Once you have developed that kind of philosophical outlook, then you will be able to situate your understanding of karma within that framework, since the karmic laws are a particular instance of this overall general causal principle.

Similarly, when you have a deep understanding of the other two dimensions of dependent origination – the dependence of parts and whole, and the interdependence between perception and existence – your view will deepen, and you will appreciate that there is a disparity between the way things appear to you and the way they actually are. What appears as some kind of autonomous, objective reality out there does not really fit with the actual nature of reality.

Once we appreciate that fundamental disparity between appearance and reality, we gain a certain insight into the way our emotions work, and how we react to events and objects. Underlying the strong emotional responses we have to situations, we see that there is an assumption that some kind of independently existing reality exists out there. In this way, we develop an insight into the various functions of the mind and the different levels of consciousness within us. We also grow to understand that although certain types of mental or emotional states seem so real, and although objects appear to be so vivid, in reality they are mere illusions. They do not really exist in the way we think they do.

It is through this type of reflection and analysis that we will be able to gain an insight into what in technical Buddhist language is called 'the origin of suffering', in other words, those emotional experiences that lead to confusion and misapprehension, and which afflict the mind. When this is combined with an understanding of the interdependent nature of reality at the subtlest level, then we also gain insight into what we call 'the empty nature of reality', by which we mean the way each and every object and event arises only as a combination of many factors, and has no independent or autonomous existence.

Our insight into emptiness will, of course, help us to understand that any ideas that are based on the contrary view, that things exist intrinsically and independently, are misapprehensions. They are misunderstandings of the nature of reality. We realize that they have no valid grounding either in reality or in our own valid experience, whereas the empty nature of reality has a valid grounding both in logical reasoning and in our experience. Gradually, we come to appreciate that it is possible to arrive at a state of knowledge where such misapprehension is eliminated completely; that is the state of cessation.

In *Clear Words* (*Prasannapada*), Chandrakirti states that if one can posit emptiness, then one can posit the world of dependent origination. If one can posit that, then one can posit the causal relationship between suffering and its origin. Once one accepts this, then one can also conceive of and accept the possibility that there could be an end to suffering. If one can do that, argues Chandrakirti, then one can also accept that it is possible for individuals to realize and actualize that state. Finally, of course, one can conceive of buddhas who have actually perfected that state of cessation.

The point is that by developing a profound understanding of the principle of dependent origination, we can understand both the truth of the subtle origins of suffering, and the truth of cessation. This is the meaning of Buddha's statement, that by understanding dependent origination, we see the Dharma. In this way we can see the truth of cessation and the path that leads to that cessation. Once we understand these, we are able to conceive that it is possible for Sangha members to realize and actualize these states, and for buddhas to perfect them. Finally, we come to some understanding of what buddhahood really means.

The Two Truths

Now in order to develop a comprehensive understanding of the Four Noble Truths, I think it is also necessary to be familiar with the Two Truths, conventional or relative truth, and ultimate truth. Here you must keep in mind that I explain them from the perspective of the Madhyamaka or 'Middle Way' School of Buddhism. Of course, the concept of Two Truths is not confined to this school alone. You can find the concept of Two Truths in other Buddhist schools of thought, and also in some non-Buddhist Indian philosophies. Here, however, I take the Madhyamaka view.

So how can we develop a personal understanding of the fundamental Buddhist doctrine of the Two Truths? By coming to know our everyday world of lived experience, we appreciate what is known as *samvaharasatya*, the world of conventional reality, where the causal principle operates. If we accept the reality of this world as conventional, then we can accept the empty nature of this world which, according to Buddhism, is the ultimate truth, the *paramarthasatya*. The relationship between these two aspects of reality is important. The world of appearance is used not so much as a contrast or an opposite to the world of ultimate truth, but rather as the evidence, the very basis on which the ultimate nature of reality is established.

Only when you have an understanding of the nature and relationship of these Two Truths are you in a position to fully understand the meaning of the Four Noble Truths. And once you understand the Four Noble Truths, then you have a sound foundation on which to develop a good understanding of what is meant by Taking Refuge in the Three Jewels.

Questions

Q: What is the difference between individuals gaining insights and the buddhas' perfection of those insights?

HHDL: Let us take the example of gaining insight into the subtle impermanence and momentary nature of all things and events.

For an individual who starts with an understanding of things as being permanent, at the initial stage his or her grasping at the permanence of things could be quite strong and intense. Now in order to loosen that grip you need some form of critical reasoning which, even if it only casts a doubt in the person's mind as to the permanence of things, can in itself make an impact because it has at least had the effect of loosening the grip on the idea that things are permanent or eternal.

However, that is not enough. You need the further reinforcement of more critical reasoning to point you towards the impermanence of things. Even that is not enough. You will need yet more conviction than this, and that can be gained through constant reflection, which can lead to what is known as the inferential understanding of impermanence.

The process is not over yet. For this understanding to have a definite impact on your behaviour, you need to gain direct insight, or intuitive experience, of the impermanence of things. That in turn needs to be further perfected, because the point is that our grasping at permanence is so deeply embedded in our consciousness that just one single insight is not enough to dispel it. It requires a long process of deepening our insight, so that eventually even the smallest tendency to grasp at permanence has been eradicated.

The process would be the same in the case of insight into the emptiness of things, or of any other principle in fact.

However, there are certain aspects of the spiritual path which have less to do with experiences related to knowledge, and more to do with the enhancement of our good heart. For the latter, at the initial stage, you have to develop some intellectual understanding of what compassion is, of course, and you have to have some notion of how it could be enhanced. Then, as a result of your practice, you may gain some kind of simulated experience of your good heart. For example, when you sit and reflect on it, you may arouse your compassion, but that compassion is not long-lasting or pervasive, and does not permeate your very being. So what is needed is a further deepening of that experience so that your compassion becomes spontaneous, so it is no longer dependent upon intellectual simulation. It has to become a truly spontaneous response to occasions that demand that response. That experience of compassion can be further deepened again, until it becomes universal. So this is a different aspect of the path, which again entails a long process.

These two aspects of the path are known in traditional Buddhist terms as the Method Aspect and the Insight or Wisdom Aspect, and both must go hand in hand. For insight to be enhanced and deepened, you need the complementary factor of bodhichitta from the Method Aspect. Similarly, in order to enhance, deepen and strengthen your realization of bodhichitta, you need the insight which grounds it. So we need an approach which combines method and wisdom.

Likewise we need an approach which combines several different methods, not an approach which relies on only one. If we take the previous case of insight into the impermanence of things, although that insight might in itself enable a person to overcome grasping at permanence, in practice you need further complementary factors in order to perfect that particular insight. This is because there are so many other fetters that constrict the mind at the same time. The person's problem is not just grasping at permanence in isolation; it is also grasping at the independent, objective reality of things, like grasping at abiding principles, and so on and so forth. All these factors can be counteracted together by developing insight into emptiness.

So what we are dealing with here is the very complex process of the progression of an individual's consciousness towards perfection.

Q: Can you say more about exactly what is meant by Going for Refuge?
HHDL: I feel that the essence of Going for Refuge is the development of a deep conviction in the efficacy of the Dharma as a means to liberation, as well as a deep aspiration or desire to attain that liberation.

Generally speaking, Buddha is said to be the teacher who shows us the path, Dharma is the actual object of Refuge, and the Sangha are your companions on the path. So therefore a deep conviction in the Dharma is a precondition for developing deep faith and respect in the Buddha and the Sangha.

In his Commentary on the Compendium of Valid Cognition (*Pramanavarttika*), Dharmakirti tries to rationally prove the validity and reliability of the fact that Buddha is an enlightened teacher. He defends his argument by subjecting Buddha's own teaching to profound scrutiny, and by demonstrating the reliability of his teaching on the Four Noble Truths because it is grounded in both reasoning and valid personal experience. The point here is that we should first appreciate the truth of the Dharma, and only on that basis recognise the Buddha as a genuine teacher.

Only in relation to extremely obscure areas is the reverse logic sometimes applied; in other words, that Buddha's statements on such matters can be relied upon *because* he is a reliable teacher. This is a complex process of reasoning. In order to follow it, we actually proceed from our own conviction in the reliability of Buddha's teachings on the Four Noble Truths, which are open to critical reasoning. When we have gained personal insight into the truth of these, we develop a deep conviction in the reliability of Buddha as a teacher. Since Buddha has proven to be reliable and rational in areas that are open to reason, we have the confidence to take Buddha's testimony on trust in other areas which we find more obscure.

Taking Refuge in the Three Jewels therefore derives its full meaning from the act of Taking Refuge in the Dharma.

Q: What is the purpose of Taking Refuge in a ritual or ceremony if one can take refuge within one's own heart alone?
HHDL: In Buddhism we have a number of different precepts or vows. For example, there are bodhisattva vows, tantric vows, pratimoksha vows (monastic vows), lay person's precepts, and so on. It is said that you can take bodhisattva vows in front of a representation of the Buddha (a statue or painting, for example) and do not need to take them from another living person. However, it is necessary to take Vajrayana and pratimoksha vows from another living person, because you need an unbroken continuum. Perhaps one of the reasons for this is that taking vows in the presence of a master or other living person brings a greater sense of commitment. It reinforces your own conscience, and gives a sense of personal obligation. If you wish to pursue the reasons for this further, then I must admit we would have to defer the question to the Buddha himself.

Q: If we see someone engaging in a wrong action which will lead to their suffering, should we try to prevent them from carrying it out, or would that be imposing on their karma? In other words, is it better for us to experience our own suffering so we can learn from it?

HHDL: As you know, a practising Buddhist is deliberately engaged in a way of life that is dedicated to helping others. Here we should know that, in the Buddhist sense, we are talking about helping others find their own liberation through engaging in the right path; that is, engaging in a way of life that accords with the karmic law, where the person avoids negative actions and engages in positive actions. So generally speaking, when a Buddhist sees others engaging in wrong actions, it is right to try to stop them from doing so.

However, this does raise several questions. To what extent can we impose our own morality, or our own sets of values, on to another person? We might even wonder whether the Buddha's prescription to his followers to live their lives according to the moral discipline of avoiding the Ten Negative Actions[7] is also a way of imposing *his* set of moral values on us.

It is useful to remember that one important principle in Buddhism is the need to be sensitive to individual context. There is a story which illustrates this point well.

Shariputra, one of the chief disciples of the Buddha, knew that if he were to give the basic teachings on the Shravakayana to a group of five hundred potential disciples, these disciples would without doubt gain insight into the truth and become Arhats. However, the bodhisattva named Manjushri intervened, and instead taught them the Mahayana doctrine of emptiness. These five hundred disciples understood what he taught as a doctrine of total nihilism, denying the validity and reality of everything. They all developed wrong views on the nature of the path and reality, and as a result it is said that they created karmic actions that led them to take rebirth in the lower realms of existence.

So Shariputra sought out the Buddha straightaway, arguing that if Manjushri had let him guide these five hundred people, they would have at least attained high levels of realization, if not full enlightenment. The Buddha responded by saying that in fact Manjushri had applied the principle of skilful means. Manjushri knew that in the short term these people would create negative actions through their wrong views, but, at the same time, he also knew that because the doctrine of emptiness had been implanted in their consciousness, those seeds would later ripen and would lead them to buddhahood. So in effect, their path to buddhahood had been shortened.

The moral that we can draw from this story is that until we reach the state of full enlightenment ourselves, it is very difficult to judge what is, and what is not, the right response to a given situation. We should simply do our best to be sensitive to each particular situation when we are interacting with others.

Q: Your Holiness, it is a well-known fact that you are a very busy person with many demands on your time. Could you advise a lay person with home, family and work demands, on how to develop a systematic pattern of Dharma practice?
HHDL: My Western friends often ask me for the quickest, easiest, most effective – and cheapest – way of practising Dharma! I think to find such a way is impossible! Maybe that is a sign of failure!

We should realize that practising the Dharma is actually something that needs to be done twenty-four hours of the day. That's why we make a distinction between actual meditation sessions and post-meditation periods, the idea being that both while you are in the meditative session and also when you are out of it, you should be fully within the realm of Dharma practice.

In fact, one could say that the post-meditation periods are the real test of the strength of your practice. During formal meditation, in a sense you are recharging your batteries, so that when you come out of the session you are better equipped to deal with the demands of your everyday life. The very purpose of recharging a battery is to enable it to run something, isn't it? Similarly, once you have equipped yourself through whatever practices you engage in, as a human being you can't avoid the daily routines of life, and it is during these periods that you should be able to live according to the principles of your Dharma practice.

Of course at the initial stage, as a beginner, you do need periods of concentrated meditation so that you have a base from which you can begin. This is certainly crucial. But once you have established that base, then you will be able to adopt a way of life where your daily activity is at least in accord with the principles of the Dharma. So all this points to the importance of making an effort. Without some effort, there is no way that we can integrate the principles of Dharma in our lives.

For a serious practitioner, the most serious effort is necessary. Just a few short prayers, a little chanting, and some mantra recitation with a mala [rosary] are not sufficient. Why not? Because this cannot transform your mind. Our negative emotions are so powerful that constant effort is needed in order to counteract them. If we practise constantly, then we can definitely change.

Q: *What is the relationship between relative compassion and absolute compassion?*
HHDL: There are different ways of understanding the meaning of compassion according to whether you approach it from the Mahayana or the Vajrayana point of view. For example, although the Vajrayana uses the same word for compassion, *karuna*, as the Mahayana, it has a totally different meaning.

Perhaps this question is related to another distinction made in the scriptures between two levels of compassion. At the first level, compassion is simulated. This is the initial stage, when you need to practise certain contemplations in order to generate compassion. As a result of this practice you reach the second level, at which compassion becomes natural and spontaneous. This is one of the ways of understanding the difference between relative and absolute compassion.

1. The first gathering to bring together leaders of the major world faiths and environmental leaders took place in Assisi, Italy, in 1986 and was organized by the Worldwide Fund for Nature.

2. 'No-soul' and 'no-self' are translations of the Sanskrit term, *anatman*. This theory is the third of the Four Seals which distinguish Buddhism from other philosophies and religions. The Four Seals are: all composite phenomena are impermanent; all contaminated phenomena are by nature unsatisfactory; all phenomena are empty of self-existence; and nirvana is true peace.

3. Dependent origination, or dependent arising, are translations of the Sanskrit *pratityasamutpada*. It is the natural law that all phenomena arise 'dependent upon' their own causes 'in connection with' their individual conditions. Everything arises exclusively due to and dependent upon the coincidence of causes and conditions without which they cannot possibly appear.

4. A buddha is literally someone who is awakened (from Sanskrit *bodhi*, awake) so buddhahood is the awakened state.

5. 'Cessation' is a technical term meaning 'the complete cessation of suffering'. Samsara refers to the cycle of suffering, and the cessation of that cycle is commonly identified as nirvana.

6. See *Majjhima Nikaya I*, p. 190–191, Pali Text Society. See also the *Pratityamutpada Sutra*.

7. The Ten Non-virtuous Actions we should avoid are: killing, stealing, sexual misconduct (three of the body), lying, slander, irresponsible chatter, verbal abuse (four of speech), covetousness, vindictiveness, and holding wrong views (three of the mind).

one

Introducing the Four Noble Truths

Now let us turn to the Buddhist teaching on the Four Noble Truths. The first question we might ask is why these Truths are considered to be so fundamental, and why, in fact, Buddha taught them at all.

In order to answer this, we have to relate the Four Noble Truths to our own experience as individual human beings. It is a fact – a natural fact of life – that each one of us has an innate desire to seek happiness and to overcome suffering. This is something very instinctive, and we do not need to prove it is there. Happiness is something that we all aspire to achieve, and of course we naturally have a right to fulfil that aspiration. In the same way, suffering is something everybody wishes to avoid, and we also have the right to try to overcome suffering. So if this aspiration to achieve happiness and overcome suffering is our natural state of being, and our natural quest, the question is how we should go about fulfilling that aspiration.

This leads us to the teachings on the Four Noble Truths, which provide an understanding of the relationship between two sets of events: causes and their effects. On one side we have suffering, but suffering does not come from nowhere, it arises as a result of its own causes and conditions. On the other side we have happiness, which also arises from its own particular set of causes and conditions.

Now when we speak of happiness in Buddhism, our understanding of it is not confined to a state of feeling. Certainly cessation (the total cessation of suffering) is not a state of feeling, and yet we could say that cessation is the highest form of happiness because it is, by definition, complete freedom from suffering. Here again cessation, or true happiness, does not come into being from nowhere or without any cause. This is a subtle point, of course, because from the Buddhist perspective cessation is not a conditioned event, so it cannot be said to be actually produced, or caused, by anything. However, the actualization or attainment of cessation does depend on the path and on an individual's effort. You cannot attain cessation without making an effort. In this sense we can therefore say that the path that leads to cessation is the cause of cessation.

The teachings on the Four Noble Truths clearly distinguish two sets of causes and effects: those causes which produce suffering, and those which produce happiness. By showing us how to distinguish these in our own lives, the teachings aim at nothing less than to enable us to fulfil our deepest aspiration – to be happy and to overcome suffering.

Once we have realized that this is why Buddha taught the Four Noble Truths, we might go on to ask ourselves the reason for their specific sequence: why are the Four Noble Truths taught in a particular order, starting with suffering, continuing with the origin of suffering, and so on? On this point we should understand that the order in which the Four Noble Truths are taught has nothing to do with the order in which things arise in reality. Rather, it is related to the way an individual should go about practising the Buddhist path, and attain realizations based on that practice.

In the *Uttaratantra*, Maitreya states that there are four stages to curing an illness.

> Just as the disease need be diagnosed, its cause eliminated, a healthy
> state achieved and the remedy implemented, so also should suffering,
> its causes, its cessation and the path be known, removed, attained and
> undertaken.[1]

Maitreya uses the analogy of a sick person to explain the way in which
realizations based on the Four Noble Truths can be attained. In order
for a sick person to get well, the first step is that he or she must know
that he is ill, otherwise the desire to be cured will not arise. Once you
have acknowledged that you are sick, then naturally you will try to
find out what led to it and what makes your condition even worse.
When you have identified these, you will gain an understanding of
whether or not the illness can be cured, and a wish to be free from the
illness will arise in you. In fact this is not just a mere wish, because
once you have recognised the conditions that led to your illness, your
desire to be free of it will be much stronger since that knowledge will
give you a confidence and conviction that you can overcome the illness. With that conviction, you will want to take all the medications
and remedies necessary.

In the same way, unless you know that you are suffering, your
desire to be free from suffering will not arise in the first place. So the
first step we must take as practising Buddhists is to recognize our present state as *duhkha* or suffering, frustration and unsatisfactoriness.
Only then will we wish to look into the causes and conditions that
give rise to suffering.

It is very important to understand the context of the Buddhist
emphasis on recognizing that we are all in a state of suffering, otherwise there is a danger we could misunderstand the Buddhist outlook,
and think that it involves rather morbid thinking, a basic pessimism
and almost an obsessiveness about the reality of suffering. The reason

why Buddha laid so much emphasis on developing insight into the nature of suffering is because there is an alternative to suffering – there is a way out, it is actually possible to free oneself from it. This is why it is so crucial to realize the nature of suffering, because the stronger and deeper your insight into suffering is, the stronger your aspiration to gain freedom from it becomes. So the Buddhist emphasis on the nature of suffering should be seen within this wider perspective, where there is an appreciation of the possibility of complete freedom from suffering. If we had no concept of liberation, then to spend so much time reflecting on suffering would be utterly pointless.

We could say that the two sets of causes and effects I mentioned earlier refer, on the one hand, to the process of an unenlightened existence, which relates to the causal chain between suffering and its origins, and on the other hand to the process of an enlightened existence which pertains to the causal links between the path and true cessation. When the Buddha elaborated on these two processes, he taught what is called the doctrine of the Twelve Links of Dependent Origination, or Twelve Nidanas.[2]

The nidanas are the twelve links in the cycle of existence, which goes from ignorance, to volition, to consciousness, and so on, all the way to old age and death. When the causal process of an unenlightened existence is described in detail – that is, a life which is led within the framework of suffering and its origin – then the sequence of the Twelve Links begins with ignorance, and proceeds with volition, consciousness and so on. This sequence describes how an individual sentient being, as a result of certain causes and conditions, enters into the process of unenlightened existence.

However, if that same individual engages in certain spiritual practices, he or she can reverse this process, and the alternative sequence is that of the process which leads to enlightenment. For example, if the continuum of ignorance comes to an end then the continuum of volitional actions will cease. If that ceases, then the consciousness that serves as the support for such actions will cease; and so on.

You can see that the teachings on the Twelve Links of Dependent Origination are in some sense an elaboration on the two sets of causes and conditions described by the Four Noble Truths.

1. The Changeless Nature, translation of the *Uttaratantra* by Ken and Katia Holmes, Karma Drubgyud Darjay Ling, UK, 1985. Page 135. The *Uttaratantra* is also known as the *Ratnagotravibhaga*.

2. The Twelve Links of Dependent Origination form the twelve-fold cycle of causal connections which binds beings to samsaric existence and thus perpetuates suffering. These Links are depicted around the famous Buddhist Wheel of Life, which illustrates the six realms of samsara and their various causes. The Links are, going clockwise around the Wheel: ignorance, volition or karmic formations, consciousness, name and form, the six bases of consciousness, contact feeling, desire, attachment, becoming, birth and old age and death. See *The Meaning of Life from a Buddhist Perspective* by His Holiness the Dalai Lama, translated and edited by Jeffrey Hopkins, Wisdom Publications, 1992.

t w o

The Truth of Suffering

The first of the Four Noble Truths is the Truth of Suffering.

The various philosophical schools of Buddhism interpret the word 'truth' in different ways. For example, there is a fundamental difference between the Prasangika-Madhyamaka school and the Shravakayana schools in the way they distinguish ordinary beings from Arya or superior beings. The Shravakayana makes the distinction on the basis of whether or not a person has gained direct intuitive insight into the Four Noble Truths. The Prasangika-Madhyamikas do not accept this criterion, because they hold that even ordinary beings can have direct intuitive realizations of the Four Noble Truths. However I will not go into these arguments here because it would complicate my explanation.

Instead, we will turn straightaway to the meaning of *duhkha* or suffering. In this context, duhkha is the ground or basis of painful experience, and refers generally to our state of existence as conditioned by karma, delusions and afflictive emotions. As Asanga states in the *Compendium of Knowledge* (*Abhidharmasamuchchaya*), the concept of duhkha must embrace both the environment where we live and the individual beings living within it.

The Three Realms of Suffering

In order to understand the environment in which unenlightened beings live, we must look briefly at Buddhist cosmology.[1] According to the Buddhist teachings, there are Three Realms of existence: the Desire Realm, the Form Realm, and the Formless Realm.[2]

The difficulty here, for most of us, is how to understand these Three Realms. In particular, how should we conceive of form realms and formless realms? It is not enough to simply say that Buddha talked about these in the scriptures – that alone is not a sufficient reason for a Buddhist to accept their existence. Perhaps the most helpful approach is to understand these realms in terms of different levels of consciousness. For example, according to Buddhism, the very distinction between enlightened existence and unenlightened existence is made on the basis of the respective levels of consciousness. A person whose mind is undisciplined and untamed is in the state of samsara or suffering; whereas someone whose mind is disciplined and tamed is in the state of nirvana, or ultimate peace.

We also find that the Buddhist distinction between ordinary and Arya beings is made on the basis of their respective levels of consciousness or realization. Anyone who has gained direct intuitive realization of emptiness, or the ultimate nature of reality, is said to be an Arya according to Mahayana, and anyone who has not gained that realization is called an ordinary being. In relation to the Three Realms, the subtler the level of consciousness an individual attains, the subtler the realm of existence he can inhabit.

For example, if a person's ordinary mode of being is very much within the context of desire and attachment – that is to say that he tends to develop attachment to whatever he perceives, like desirable forms or pleasant sensations and so on – then such attachment to physical objects, thought processes and sensory experiences leads to a form of existence which is confined within the Desire Realm, both now and in the future. At the same time, there are people who have transcended attachment to objects of immediate perception and to physical sensations, but who are attached to the inner states of joy or bliss. That type of person creates causes that will lead him or her to future rebirths where physical existence has a much more refined form.

Furthermore, there are those who have transcended attachment not only to physical sensations but to pleasurable inner sensations of joy and bliss, too. They tend more towards a state of equanimity. Their level of consciousness is much subtler than the other two, but they are still attached to a particular mode of being. The grosser levels of their mind can lead to the Fourth Level of the Form Realm, while the subtler attachment towards equanimity leads to the Formless Realms. So this is the way we relate the Three Realms to levels of consciousness.

On the basis of this cosmology, Buddhism talks about the infinite process of the universe, coming into being and going through a process of dissolution before again coming into being. This process has to be understood in relation to the Three Realms of existence. According to the Sarvastivadin Abhidharma literature[3] (the Buddhist discourses on metaphysics and psychology which serve as a reference in Tibetan Buddhism), it is from the Third Level of the Form Realm downwards that the world is subject to the continuous process of arising and dissolution. From the Fourth Level of the Form Realm upwards, which includes the Formless Realm, the world is beyond this process which we could call the evolution of the physical universe.

This infinite process of evolution is very similar to the modern scientific notion of the Big Bang. If the scientific cosmological theory of the Big Bang accepts only one Big Bang as *the* beginning of everything, then of course that would not fit with basic Buddhist cosmology. In this case, Buddhists would have to bite their nails and come up with some way of explaining how the Big Bang does not contradict the Buddhist idea of the evolutionary process of the universe. However, if the Big Bang theory does not entail only one Big Bang at the beginning, but accepts a multiplicity of Big Bangs, then that would correspond very well to the Buddhist understanding of the evolutionary process.

The Sarvastivadin Abhidharma also discusses the precise ways in which the universe dissolves at the end of each cycle. When the physical universe is destroyed by fire it is destroyed only below the first level of the Form Realm; when it is destroyed by water it dissolves from the second level of the Form Realm downwards; when it is destroyed by wind, it is destroyed from the third level of the Form Realm downwards. In Buddhist cosmology, therefore, the evolution of the physical universe is understood in terms of the four elements of fire, water, wind and earth. In general, we usually add space to this list, making a total of five elements. A complex discussion on the elemental mechanics of dissolution can be found not only in the Abhidharma but also in the *Uttaratantra*. These explanations seem to be very similar to modern scientific theories.

Having said this, what is stated in the Abhidharma literature does not always have to be taken literally. According to the Abhidharma, for example, the structure of the universe is based on the model of a Mount Meru in the centre, surrounded by four 'continents'. We also find that many of the Abhidharmic descriptions of the size of the sun and moon contradict modern scientific explanations. Given that scientific experiments have proved these claims to be wrong, we will have to accept the conclusion of the scientists on these points.

So here I have outlined very briefly how Buddhism understands the evolution of the physical universe, or, in a broad sense, the environment. As for the sentient beings that inhabit these environments,

Buddhism accepts many different types. There are beings with bodily forms and beings which are perceived as formless. Even in the world with which we are familiar, there are many beings which are perceptible to our senses and some which are not, like those of the spirit world for example.

Generally speaking, the Buddhist understanding is that birth as a human being is one of the most ideal forms of existence because it is conducive to practising Dharma. So compared to human beings, spirits would in fact be considered inferior because that form of existence is less effective for pursuing the practice of Dharma. Spirits may have certain abilities that are not open to us, like certain powers of precognition or some supernatural powers, but the fact remains that they are part of this world where human beings also live. All beings in this world are under the control of delusion and afflictive emotions. In some sense one could say that they are actually the products of delusion and afflictive emotions.

Lama Tsongkhapa describes very vividly the unenlightened existence of sentient beings in samsara. He uses the analogy of someone being tied up very tightly by the ropes of negative karma, delusions, afflictive emotions and thoughts. Encased in this tight net of ego and self-grasping, they are tossed around aimlessly by the currents of fluctuating experiences, of suffering and pain.[4] This is what samsaric life is like.

Three Types of Suffering

So now the question is, what is duhkha? What is suffering? Buddhism describes three levels or types of suffering. The first is called 'the suffering of suffering', the second, 'the suffering of change', and the third is 'the suffering of conditioning'.

When we talk about the first type, the suffering of suffering, we are talking in very conventional terms of experiences which we would all identify as suffering. These experiences are painful. In Buddhism there are four main experiences of this type of suffering which are considered to be fundamental to life in samsara: the sufferings of birth, sickness, ageing and death. The significance of recognizing these states as forms of suffering, and the importance of this recognition as a catalyst of the spiritual quest, is very strongly demonstrated in Buddha's own life story. According to the story, when he was the young Prince Siddhartha, Buddha is said to have caught sight of a sick person, an old person, and a dead person being carried away. The impact of seeing this suffering apparently led him to the realization that so long as he was not free of the infinite process of birth, he would always be subject to these other three sufferings. Later, the sight of a spiritual aspirant is supposed to have made the Buddha fully aware that there is a possibility of freedom from this cycle of suffering.

So in Buddhism there is an understanding that so long as we are subject to the process of rebirth, all other forms of suffering are natural consequences of that initial starting point. We could characterize our life as being within the cycle of birth and death, and sandwiched in between these two, as it were, are the various sufferings related to illness and ageing.

The second level of suffering, the suffering of change, refers to experiences we ordinarily identify as pleasurable. However, in reality, as long as we are in an unenlightened state, all our joyful experiences are tainted and ultimately bring suffering.

Why does Buddhism claim that experiences which are apparently pleasurable are ultimately states of suffering? The point is that we perceive them as states of pleasure or joy only because, in comparison to painful experiences, they appear as a form of relief. Their pleasurable status is only relative. If they were truly joyful states in themselves, then just as painful experiences increase the more we indulge in the causes that lead to pain, likewise, the more we engage in the causes that give rise to pleasurable experience, our pleasure or joy should intensify; but this is not the case.

On an everyday level, for example, when you have good food, nice clothes, attractive jewellery and so on, for a short time you feel really marvellous. Not only do you enjoy a feeling of satisfaction, but when you show your things to others, they share in it too. But then one day passes, one week passes, one month passes, and the very same object that once gave you such pleasure might simply cause you frustration. That is the nature of things – they change. The same also applies to fame. At the beginning you might think to yourself, 'Oh! I'm so happy! Now I have a good name, I'm famous!' But after some time, it could be that all you feel is frustration and dissatisfaction. The same sort of change can happen in friendships and in sexual relationships. At the beginning you almost go mad with passion, but later that very passion can turn to hatred and aggression, and, in the worst cases, even lead to murder. So that is the nature of things. If you look carefully, everything beautiful and good, everything that we consider desirable, brings us suffering in the end.

Finally, we come to the third type of suffering, the suffering of conditioning. This addresses the main question: why is this the nature of things? The answer is, because everything that happens in samsara is due to ignorance. Under the influence or control of ignorance, there is no possibility of a permanent state of happiness. Some kind of trouble, some kind of problem, always arises. So long as we remain under the power of ignorance, that is, our fundamental misapprehension or confusion about the nature of things, then sufferings come one after another, like ripples on water.

The third level of suffering, therefore, refers to the bare fact of our unenlightened existence, which is under the influence of this fundamental confusion and of the negative karmas to which confusion gives rise. The reason it is called the suffering of conditioning is because this state of existence serves as the basis not only for painful experiences in this life, but also for the causes and conditions of suffering in the future.

Dharmakirti's *Commentary on the Compendium of Valid Cognition* (*Pramanavarttika*) and Aryadeva's *Four Hundred Verses on the Middle Way* (*Chatuhshatakashastrakarika*) both offer a useful way of looking at this third level of suffering, and help deepen our understanding of it. Both works lay the emphasis on reflecting upon the subtle level of the transient, impermanent nature of reality.

It is important to bear in mind that there are two levels of meaning here. One can understand impermanence in terms of how something arises, stays for a while, and then disappears. This level of impermanence can be understood quite easily. We should add that on this level, the dissolution of something requires a secondary condition which acts as a catalyst to destroy its continuity. However, there is also a second, more subtle understanding of transience. From this more subtle perspective, the obvious process of change we have just described is merely the effect of a deeper, underlying and dynamic process of change. At a deeper level, everything is changing from moment to moment, constantly. This process of momentary change is not due to a secondary condition that arises to destroy something, but rather the very cause that led a thing to arise is also the cause of its destruction. In other words, within the cause of its origin lies the cause of its cessation.

Momentariness should thus be understood in two ways. First, in terms of the three moments of existence of any entity – in the first instant, it arises; in the second instant, it stays; in the third instant, it dissolves. Second, in terms of each instant itself. An instant is not static; as soon as it arises, it moves towards its own cessation.

Since everything arises complete from the outset, the birth of things comes together with the seed or potential for their dissolution. In this respect, one could say that their cessation does not depend on any secondary, further condition. Therefore, in Buddhism, all phenomena are said to be 'other-powered', that is, they are under the control of their causes.

Once you have developed this understanding of the transient nature of phenomena, you are able to situate the understanding you have of duhkha within that context, and reflect upon your life as an individual in this samsaric world. You know that since the world has come into being as a result of its own causes and conditions, it too must be other-powered. In other words it must be under the control of the causal processes that led to its arising. However, in the context of samsara, the causes that we are referring to here are nothing other than our fundamental confusion or ignorance (*marigpa* in Tibetan), and the delusory states to which confusion gives rise. We know that so long as we are under the domination of this fundamental confusion, there is no room for lasting joy or happiness. Of course, within the Three Realms there are states which are comparatively more joyful than others. However, so long as we remain within samsara, whether in the Form Realm, the Formless Realm or the Desire Realm, there is no scope for joy to be lasting. In the final analysis, we are in a state of duhkha. This is the meaning of the third type of suffering.

Ignorance

The Sanskrit word for ignorance or confusion is *avidya*, which literally means 'not knowing'. There are several interpretations of what is meant by avidya according to the different philosophical schools and their various views of the fundamental Buddhist doctrine of *anatman* or no-self. However, the general meaning that is common to all the schools is an understanding that there lies a fundamental ignorance at the root of our existence. The reason for this is quite simple. We all know from personal experience that what we deeply aspire to gain is happiness and what we try to avoid is suffering. Yet our actions and our behaviour only lead to more suffering and not to the lasting joy and happiness that we seek. This must surely mean that we are operating within the framework of ignorance. This is how we experience the fundamental confusion at the root of our life.

One way to reflect on the nature of duhkha, according to the traditional Buddhist teachings, is to reflect on the sufferings endured in each of the six 'realms' of the samsaric world system.[5] These include the hell realms, the animal realm, the realm of pretas or hungry ghosts, and so on. For some people, such reflections may spur them to deepen their quest for freedom from suffering. However, for many other people, including myself, it can be more effective to reflect on our own human suffering. Although Buddhism teaches that human life is one of the most positive of all forms of life, since human beings have the potential to gain perfect enlightenment, it is not always that joyful. We are subject to the unavoidable sufferings of birth, death, ageing and sickness. In addition, when one reflects on the fact that life is conditioned and dominated by confusion, and the delusory emotions and thoughts to which confusion gives rise, then for someone like myself it seems much more effective to recognize this than to think about the sufferings of other realms.

As I mentioned before, the Buddhist scriptures describe the causal process through which ignorance gives rise to volitional acts, which in turn give rise to a birth in one of the samsaric worlds, and so on, as the Twelve Links in the Chain of Dependent Origination. On this, Buddha made three observations. He said that:

Because there is this, that ensues.

Because this came into being, that came into being.

Because there is fundamental ignorance, volitional acts come into being.[6]

When commenting upon these three statements, Asanga explains in the *Compendium of Knowledge* that Three Conditions are necessary for anything to arise, and I think an understanding of these would be quite useful at this point.

Because there is this, that ensues

Asanga explained that the significance of the first statement is that all phenomena come into being because they have causes. One could say there is an infinite causal chain. It is not as if there were a first cause, or a 'beginning' point in time, from which everything arose. Asanga referred to that observation or qualification as the first condition: the **Condition of the Existence of a Cause**.

Because this came into being, that came into being

When commenting on the second statement, Asanga introduced what he called the **Condition of Impermanence**. The meaning of this is that the mere fact that something exists is not sufficient for it to produce an effect. For something to have the potential to produce an effect, it must itself be subject to causation; in other words, it must come into being itself as a result of other causes. Hence we have an infinity of causes. So mere existence alone does not give rise to consequences; a cause should not only exist, it should also be impermanent and subject to causation.

Because there is fundamental ignorance, volitional acts come into
being

Asanga's comment on this mentions a further qualification that is
needed for a cause to produce an effect, which he calls the **Condition
of Potentiality**. The idea is that it is not sufficient for a cause to exist
and to be impermanent for it to produce a particular result. It is not
the case that everything can produce everything or anything. There
must be some kind of natural correlation between a cause and its
effect. For example, because the nature of our life is suffering we desire
happiness, yet out of ignorance we create more suffering for ourselves,
and this is because suffering is the root of our life. The result we
obtain thus correlates with its cause.

So to summarize, Three Conditions are necessary for anything to
arise: a cause should exist, it should be impermanent, and it should
correlate with the effect.

In view of this, how should we understand the causal relationship
between, say, ignorance and volitional acts? Buddhism pursues a rigorous
analysis of causal relationships in general, and the scriptures contain
many discussions on the different types of causes and conditions.
However, there are principally two types of cause one is known as the
material or substantial cause, and the other as the contributory cause. By
material cause we mean the very stuff that turns into the effect, so we can
talk for example about the physical continuum of a physical entity. Many
other factors are necessary to allow the transition to take place between a
cause and its effect, and these are called the contributory causes.

Furthermore, there are different ways in which conditions can
effect a result. These have more to do with the complex functioning

of the mind. The scriptures identify five types of condition, such as the objective condition, which refers to the object of perception; the sensory organs that give rise to sensory perception; the immediately preceding condition, which is the earlier continuum of your consciousness; and so on. So you can see that the Buddhist understanding of causation is highly complex.

Let us take the example of fire. What would the material cause of fire be? We could say that a potential exists within the fuel that is used to make a fire, which then becomes the fire. In the case of consciousness, the issue is more complex. For example, it is obvious that we need the physical sensory organs for sensory perceptions to take place. Of course, the physical basis of consciousness would also include the nervous system, although in the classic Buddhist scriptures there is hardly any discussion of this, and it is perhaps something that needs to be added to Buddhist theories of epistemology and psychology. However, the substantial cause of consciousness would not be these physical entities. It has to be understood in terms of its own continuum, be it in the form of a potential or propensity or whatever. This is a very difficult topic, but perhaps we can say that the substantial cause of consciousness can be understood as the continuum of the subtle consciousness, although we should be careful not to end up in a position which implies that the material cause of anything is exactly the same as the thing itself. This would be untenable. We cannot maintain the position, for instance, that the substantial causes of sensory perceptions are always sensory perceptions, because sensory consciousnesses are gross levels of consciousness and are contingent on the physical organs of the individual, whereas the continuum should be understood on the level of the subtle consciousness. So perhaps we could say that the substantial causes of consciousness are present in the form of a potential rather than as actual conscious states.

Consciousness

When we talk about consciousness, or *shes pa* in Tibetan, we are not talking about a single, unitary, monolithic entity that is 'out there'. We are referring, of course, to the mental consciousness which is the sixth consciousness according to Buddhist psychology.[7]

Generally speaking, when we try to investigate our mind through introspection, we find that it tends to be dominated either by discursive thoughts or by feelings and sensations. So let us try to examine how feelings and discursive thoughts occur within the mind.

Feelings, of course, can be considered in relation to two different dimensions of reality. We can speak about them purely at the physical level, as sensations, but when we try to understand feelings in terms of mental consciousness the issue is far more complex. And although we naturally accept that there must be connections between the consciousness and the nervous system of the body, we must somehow be able to account for deeper levels of feeling as well, or what we could call tones of experience.

I would like to point out that although very little research has been carried out in this area, and despite the fact that what little exists is still at a rudimentary stage, experiments done on meditators point to a phenomenon which may be difficult to account for within the current scientific paradigm. These experiments have shown that without any voluntary physical change in the body, and without any physical movement on the part of the individual, a person can affect his or her physiological state simply by using the power of the mind through a focused, single-pointed state. The physiological changes that take place are difficult to explain according to current assumptions about human physiology.

There is no doubt that our consciousness and all our experiences are contingent upon our body, so the human mind and the human body are in some sense inextricable. Yet at the same time, I feel that research seems to point to the possibility that the human mind also has a power of its own which can be enhanced through reflection and meditation, or training of the mind. Furthermore, it is well known that there is a growing recognition within modern medicine of the power of the will in the healing process. A person's willpower affects his physiology. How is willpower developed? It can be through thinking something through and discovering the reasonable grounds for one's understanding. It can also be through meditation. In whichever way it is developed, it is now acknowledged that the will can effect physical change.

What does this mean? What seems to be accepted scientifically is that all the thoughts that occur in our mind give rise to chemical changes and movements within the brain, which are then expressed or manifested in physiological change. But does pure thought lead to such physical effects too? And is it the case that thoughts occur solely as a result of chemical changes within the body or brain? I have asked scientists on several occasions whether it would be possible for the process to begin first with just pure thought, and then, secondly, thought processes occur which give rise to chemical changes, which in turn trigger physiological effects. Most of the time their answers have indicated that since it is assumed that consciousness is contingent upon a physical base (the brain, for instance), every occurrence of thought must necessarily be accompanied or caused by chemical changes in the brain. To me, however, that assumption seems to be based more on prejudice than experimental proof. I therefore think the question is still open and further research is needed, particularly involving practitioners who engage in profound meditation.

The Vajrayana literature contains discussions of the existence of different levels of consciousness, or different subtleties of mind, and the ways in which these correspond to subtle levels of energy. I think these explanations can contribute a great deal to our understanding of the nature of mind and its functions.

So, as we saw earlier, most of our conscious mind consists either of states related with objects that we have experienced in the past – recollections of past experiences inform our present consciousness – or it consists of some kind of feeling or sensation. As a result, it is very difficult for us to glimpse the actual nature of consciousness, which is the sheer state of knowing or the luminosity of mind. One technique that we can use in order to do this is sitting meditation, through which we free our mind from thoughts of past experiences and from any form of anticipation of the future. Instead, we abide in the nowness of the present, although we cannot really talk of a 'present' consciousness.

When you are able to clear away thoughts of the past and the future, slowly you begin to get a sense of the space between the two. You learn to abide in that present moment. In that space, you begin to glimpse what we call emptiness, and if you can remain in that emptiness for longer and longer periods of time then gradually the nature of consciousness itself, which is the sheer luminosity and natural awareness of mind, will slowly dawn in you. Through repeated practice this period can be lengthened more and more, so that your awareness of the nature of consciousness becomes clearer and clearer.

However, it is important to realize that this experience of the luminosity of mind, of the nature of mind, is not a profound realization in itself. Rebirth in many of the formless realms of samsara is considered to result from abiding in such states of clarity. On the other hand, if we know how to use that initial experience of luminosity as a basis, then we can build on it by complementing our meditation with other practices, and in this way it will become truly profound.

So here I have explained how we can look at the Buddha's teaching on the Truth of Suffering. Once you have developed this kind of recognition of the duhkha nature of life, you already have some understanding that at the root of our suffering lies a fundamental ignorance. This of course leads us to the Second Truth which is the Origin of Suffering.

Questions

Q: Your Holiness, if corporeal beings are impermanent due to their complex physical nature, are spiritual beings permanent because of their lack of physical substance?

HHDL: Let us take the example of a formless being, that is, a being who, according to Buddhism, is in the Formless Realm. Unlike beings in the Desire Realm or Form Realm, that sentient being may not be subject to the natural processes of decay to which corporeal beings are subject, yet it still remains impermanent because it has a limited life-span during which it remains in the Formless Realm. Since its life there has a beginning and an end, it is still subject to the process of change.

However, if we are talking about a being who has attained the state of moksha and has become an arhat, then the situation is different. Similarly, bodhisattvas on very high levels of realization (from the eighth bodhisattva level onwards) are no longer subject to the process of ageing. In a sense one could say that from the point of view of the continuity of consciousness, there is a sense of permanence for such beings. Moreover, such beings are described in the scriptures as having a mental rather than a corporeal form. We should note that this mental form is very different from the 'mental body' that is described in Vajrayana, in relation to the after-death states, for example.

1. For a detailed treatment of Buddhist cosmology in English, see *Myriad Worlds* by

Jamgon Kongtrul, Snow Lion, 1995.

2. The human world is part of the Desire Realm. The Formless Realm is more subtle than the Form Realm, which in turn is more subtle than the Desire Realm.

3. The early teachings of Buddhism are divided into the Vinaya, or code of discipline, the Sutras, or discourses of the Buddha, and the Abhidharma which is the commentarial and philosophical literature composed by Buddhist masters. Two complete corpuses of Abhidharma literature have survived to the present day: that of the Theravada school, in Pali, and that of the Sarvastivada school, in Sanskrit. Only the Sarvastivadin Abhidharma was taught in Tibet. The chief reference on cosmology is Chapter Three of Vasubandhu's *Abhidharmakosha*, translated into English by Leo Pruden, Asian Humanities Press, Berkeley California, 1991.

4. *Three Aspects of the Path*, verse 7. See Robert Thurman's *Life and Teachings of Tsongkhapa*, Library of Tibetan Works and Archives, Dharamsala, India, 1982.

5. According to Tibetan Buddhism there are six realms in samsara, each dominated by a particular mental poison. They are: the hell realms (anger), the animal realm (ignorance), the realm of pretas or hungry ghosts (miserliness), the human realm (desire), the demi-god or Asura realm (jealousy), and the god realm (pride).

6. This statement can be found in *Majjhima Nikaya I* (p. 262, Pali Text Society) and *Majjhima III* (p. 43, Pali Text Society) and *Samyutta Nikaya II* (p. 28, Pali Text Society).

7. Buddhist psychology bases the perception process on six sense faculties: sight, hearing, smell, taste, touch and thought. Each faculty relates to a sense organ (eye, ear, nose, tongue, body, mind) and to a consciousness which functions specifically with that organ. There are thus six sense consciousnesses, the sixth one being the mental consciousness.

three

The Truth of the Origin of Suffering

In the previous chapter we looked at the fact that we all desire happiness and wish to overcome suffering, and how, despite this natural aspiration, we tend to create the conditions for more suffering because we do not know the way to create the causes for happiness. We found that at the root of this situation lies a fundamental confusion or, in Buddhist terminology, a fundamental ignorance. This confusion applies not only to the way things are but also to the way causes and effects relate to each other. Therefore, in Buddhism we talk about two types of ignorance, or *avidya*: ignorance of the laws of causality, specifically of the laws of karma, and ignorance of the ultimate nature of reality. These relate respectively to the two levels of understanding of dependent origination that we outlined in Chapter One. The first level was an understanding in terms of causal dependence, which dispels our ignorance of the laws of causality. The more profound level was an understanding in terms of the ultimate nature of reality, which dispels our fundamental ignorance.

However, this does not mean that ignorance is the only cause of our unenlightened existence. This has, of course, many other derivative causes and conditions, which are technically called *kleshas* or 'afflictive emotions and thoughts'. This is a very complex class of emotions and thoughts, described in detail in the Abhidharma literature. For example, according to Abhidharma there are six root afflictive emotions or thoughts, out of which arise 20 secondary types of emotions and thoughts. The Abhidharma therefore presents a comprehensive explanation of the whole world of thought and emotion.

There is another explanation of the process of being in samsara in the Tantric Vajrayana literature, which details the 80 types of thoughts or concepts which are indicative of our being in an unenlightened state. The Kalachakra literature, which belongs to the Vajrayana class, further identifies the causes of samsaric existence in terms of propensities or natural dispositions.

These afflictive emotions and thoughts, which arise from our fundamental delusion, give rise to volitional actions. So together, delusions and karmic actions are the origins of our suffering.

Generally speaking, afflictive emotions and thoughts are defined as those of which the mere occurrence creates immediate disturbance within our mind. They then afflict us from within.

Karma
Categories of Karmic Action

If that is the general definition of klesha, what is the definition of karma?[1] We should remember to situate karma within the context of the wider Buddhist understanding of the natural laws of causality. Karma is one particular instance of the natural causal laws that operate throughout the universe where, according to Buddhism, things and events come into being purely as a result of the combination of causes and conditions.

Karma, then, is an instance of the general law of causality. What makes karma unique is that it involves intentional action, and therefore an agent. The natural causal processes operating in the world cannot be termed karmic where there is no agent involved. In order for a causal process to be a karmic one, it must involve an individual whose intention would lead to a particular action. It is this specific type of causal mechanism which is known as karma.

So within the general field of karmic action we can talk about three different types of actions which produce corresponding effects. Actions which produce suffering and pain are generally considered negative or non-virtuous actions. Actions that lead to positive and desirable consequences, such as experiences of joy and happiness, are considered to be positive or virtuous actions. The third category includes actions which lead to experiences of equanimity, or neutral feelings and experiences; these are considered to be neutral actions, and are neither virtuous nor non-virtuous.

In terms of the actual nature of karmic actions themselves, there are principally two different types: mental acts – actions that are not necessarily manifested through physical action – and there are physical acts, which include both bodily and verbal acts. Then, from the point of view of the medium of expression of an action, we distinguish actions of the mind, actions of speech, and actions of the body. Furthermore, in the scriptures we also find discussions about karmic actions which are completely virtuous, completely non-virtuous, and those which are a mixture of the two. I feel that for many of us who practise the Dharma, most of our actions may be a mixture of the two.

If we analyse a single karmic action, we can see that there are several stages within that event. There is a beginning, which is the stage of the motivation or intention; there is the actual execution of the act; and then there is the culmination or completion of the act. According to the scriptures, the intensity and force of a karmic action vary according to the way each of these stages is carried out.

Let us take the example of a negative action. If, at the stage of motivation, the person has a very strong negative emotion like anger, and then acts on an impulse and carries out the action, but immediately afterwards feels deep regret for the action he has committed, all three stages would not be completely fulfilled. Consequently, the action would be less powerful compared to an instance where the person has acted out all stages completely – with a strong motivation, actual execution, and a sense of taking pleasure or satisfaction from the act committed. Similarly, there could be cases where the individual may have a very weak motivation but circumstances force him or her to actually commit the act. In this case, although a negative act has been committed it would be even less powerful than in our first example, because a strong motivating force was not present. So depending on the strength of the motivation, of the actual act, and of the completion, the karma produced will have corresponding degrees of intensity.

On the basis of these differences, the scriptures discuss four types of karma: karma which is carried out but not accumulated, karma which is accumulated but not carried out, karma where the act is both carried out and accumulated, and karma where there is an absence of both accumulation and the actual execution of the act. It is important to understand the significance of this point, and to appreciate that since there are different stages to every act, karmic actions themselves are composite, and their quality can be characterized as the cumulative result of each of their composing factors.

Once you appreciate this, then whenever you have the opportunity to engage in a positive action as a Dharma practitioner, it is important to ensure that at the initial stage your positive motivation is very strong, and that you have a strong intention to engage in the act. Then, while you are actually carrying out the act, you should ensure that you have given it your best, and you have put all your effort into making the action successful. Once the action is performed, it is important to ensure that you dedicate the positive karma that you have thereby created towards the well-being of all beings as well as your own attainment of enlightenment. If you can reinforce that dedication with an understanding of the ultimate nature of reality, it would be even more powerful.

Ideally, as Dharma practitioners, we should of course try to avoid engaging in any negative actions at all, but even if we do find ourselves in a situation where we are committing a non-virtuous action, it is important to make sure that at least our motivation is not strong and there is no strong emotion involved. Then, even while we are carrying out the action, if we have a strong pang of conscience, and a sense of regret or remorse, then of course the negative act will be very weak. Finally, the action should not be followed by any sense of satisfaction. We should not take pleasure in any negative action we have committed, but rather we should feel deep remorse and regret, and immediately afterwards we should purify the negativity, if possible. If we can do this, if we can live a way of life where we relate to our positive and negative actions in this way, then we will be able to follow the teachings on the law of karma much more effectively.

Although there are many different types of negative action, the Buddhist scriptures summarize them as the Ten Negative or Ten Non-virtuous Actions. There are three actions of body, four of speech, and three of mind. The three bodily negative actions are killing, stealing, and sexual misconduct; the four negative actions of speech are lying, engaging in divisive speech, using harsh words, and engaging in senseless gossip; and the three negative mental actions are covetousness, harbouring harmful thoughts and intentions, and holding wrong views. Ideally, a Dharma practitioner should live in such a way that he avoids all these negative actions if possible, and if not, then at least he should refrain from as many as he can. Leading a disciplined life and avoiding negative actions is what Buddhists understand as an ethical way of life.

Karma and the Person

How does a Buddhist practitioner actually go about trying to lead a moral life? A person's ultimate aspiration is to attain liberation from samsara, to attain spiritual freedom or enlightenment, so one of his or her principal tasks is to gain victory over the kleshas. However, there is no way that a practitioner can directly combat negative emotions and thoughts at the initial stage, so the sensible way to proceed is simply to find a way of containing the expression of the negative actions of our body, speech and mind. The first step, then, is to guard our body, speech and mind from engaging in negative actions so that we don't give in to the power and domination of our negative thoughts and emotions.

Once you have achieved this first stage, you can proceed to the second stage and tackle the root cause – the fundamental ignorance of which we spoke earlier. At this stage you are able to counteract the forces of the kleshas directly. Once you can do that, the third stage consists not simply of gaining victory over them, but also of rooting out all the propensities and imprints they have left within the psyche. This is why Aryadeva states in the *Four Hundred Verses on Madhyamaka* that a true spiritual aspirant must first overcome negative behaviour, in the middle phase must counter any grasping at self, and in the final stage should overcome all the views that bind us within the samsaric realm.[2]

As we have already seen, Buddhism explains how both the environment and the sentient beings living in that environment are produced as a result of fundamental ignorance, particularly the karma which arises from ignorance. However, we should not think that karma produces these things from out of nowhere. This is not the case. Karma is not like an eternal cause. We should realize that in order for karma to operate, and in order for it to have the potential to create its consequences, it must have a basis on which to do so. It follows that there exists a continuum of both the physical and the mental worlds. We can trace the continuum of the physical world to the beginning of a particular universe, and then we can even trace that 'beginning' to empty space. Buddhism accepts the existence of what are known as 'space particles' (*namkhai dul*), and asserts there is a stage of empty space in which the source of the material universe is in some sense contained. In the case of the mental world, we cannot say that the continuum of consciousness in sentient beings is a result of karma. Neither can we say that the unending process of the continuity of both matter and mind results from karma.

If this is the case, if the basic continuum is not produced by karma, then where does karma fit in? At what point does karma play a causal role in producing sentient beings and the natural environment in which they live? Perhaps we can say that there is a natural process in the world, and at a certain point when its evolution has reached a stage where it can affect the experiences of beings – giving rise to either painful experiences of suffering or joyful experiences of happiness – that is the point where karma enters the picture. After all, the karmic process only makes sense in relation to the experience of sentient beings.

So if we were to ask whether consciousness is produced by karma, or whether sentient beings are produced by karma, it seems the answer should be 'no'. But on the other hand, if we ask whether the human body and the human consciousness are products of karma, then the answer is 'yes' because both result from virtuous actions. This is because, when we talk about the human body and human consciousness, we are referring to a state of existence which is directly related to the painful and pleasurable experiences of an individual. Finally, if we were to ask whether or not our natural instinct to seek happiness and overcome suffering is a product of karma, it seems the answer would again be 'no'.

Karma and the Natural World

Now when we turn to the evolution of the physical universe at large, we cannot say that the natural processes of cause and effect are a product of karma. The process of cause and effect in the natural world takes place regardless of karma. Nevertheless, karma would have a role to play in determining the form that the process takes, or the direction in which it leads.

Here we should mention that from the Buddhist analytical point of view, we distinguish two realms of enquiry. One realm we could call 'natural', where only the natural process of causal laws operates, and the other is where certain properties emerge, contingent on these causal interactions. On account of this distinction we find that different avenues of reasoning are used when trying to understand the nature of the world or of reality.

For example, in Buddhist analysis we use what we call the Four Principles. The first is the *Principle of Nature*: the fact that things exist, and that causes lead to effects. We could almost say that this principle implies an acceptance of natural laws. Then we have the *Principle of Efficacy*: this deals with the way things have the capacity to produce certain results according to their nature. The third is the *Principle of Dependence*: given the first two principles, we see there is a natural dependence between things and events, between causes and effects. On the basis of these three principles, Buddhist critical analysis applies various types of reasoning to broaden or deepen our understanding of the natural world. Therefore the fourth principle we accept is the

Principle of Valid Proof: given this, that must be the case; and given that, this should be the case.

For a practising Buddhist, it is important to appreciate these principles of the natural world, so that one is in a position to utilize that knowledge to live a life that is in accord with the principles of Dharma. We could therefore say that by living according to the Dharma we would be applying the Principle of Valid Proof, in terms of the way in which we avoid negative actions and enhance virtuous actions.

So, as I mentioned earlier, the questions we now have to consider are: at what point in the causal process does karma come into the picture? and in what manner does karma interact with the process of the natural causal laws?

Perhaps we can refer to our own personal experience in order to answer these questions. Experience shows that certain actions we do in the morning, for example, will have a continuing effect even in the evening. The action will have created a certain state of mind. It will have had an impact upon our emotion and our sense of being so even though it was committed in the morning as an event that is finished, its effect still lingers on in our mind. I think the same principle operates with karma and its effects, even in the case of long-term karmic effects. This is how we understand that karma can create effects which are felt even a long time after the act was committed. According to the Buddhist explanation, of course, the impact of karma can be felt over successive lifetimes as well as in our present life.

At this point I feel that unless we complement the general explanation of the karmic process found in the Buddhist literature[3] with points from the Vajrayana literature, our understanding will not be complete. The Vajrayana explains that both the physical world and the bodies of living beings are composed of the five elements: earth, water, fire, wind, and space. Space here should be understood in terms of vacuum, of empty space, rather than as space in the technical sense of absence of obstruction. The Vajrayana literature discusses these in terms of external elements and internal elements, and shows how they are related to each other at a very profound level. Through understanding this relationship, our insight into the way karma affects the world is a much deeper one.

As we discussed earlier, the fact that consciousness exists is a natural fact. Consciousness exists; that is it. Similarly, the continuum of consciousness is also a natural principle: consciousness maintains its continuity. To this we must add that in Buddhism, there is an understanding that consciousness cannot arise from nowhere or without a cause; and, at the same time, that consciousness cannot be produced from matter. This is not to say that matter cannot affect consciousness. However, the nature of consciousness is sheer luminosity, mere experience; it is the primordial knowing faculty, and therefore it cannot be produced from matter whose nature is different. It follows that since consciousness cannot arise without a cause, and since it cannot arise from a material cause, it must come from a ceaseless continuum. It is on this premise that Buddhism accepts the existence of (beginningless) former lives.[4]

We have seen that the origin of suffering lies in both karma and ignorance, but actually ignorance is the principal origin.

Karma and the emotions

There are differences in the way each school of Buddhism understands the nature of the kleshas, corresponding to their various interpretations of the doctrine of *anatman*, or no-soul theory. For example, certain states of mind, and certain thoughts and emotions which, according to the Madhyamaka-Svatantrika and Chittamatra schools, may be considered non-delusory, are seen as delusory from the point of view of the Madhyamaka-Prasangika school. This is a very complex point, of course, and would require a lot of study.

The most important thing for us to know is that afflictive emotion is our ultimate enemy and a source of suffering. Once it develops within our mind, it immediately destroys our peace of mind, and eventually destroys our health, and even our friendships with other people. All negative activities such as killing, bullying, cheating and so forth, stem from afflictive emotion. This, therefore, is our real enemy.

An external enemy may be harmful to you today, but tomorrow could become very helpful, whereas the inner enemy is consistently destructive. Moreover, wherever you live the inner enemy is always there with you, and that makes it very dangerous. In contrast, we can often keep an external enemy at some kind of distance. In 1959, for example, we escaped from Tibet since escape was a physical possibility; but in the case of this inner enemy, whether I am in Tibet, or in the Potala, or in Dharamsala, or here in London, wherever I go it follows me. I think the inner enemy is even there in meditation; and even if I visualize a mandala, I may still find this enemy in its very centre! So this is the main point we have to realize: the real destroyer of our happiness is always there within us.

So what can we do about it? If it is not possible to work on that enemy and to eliminate it, then I think we had better forget the spiritual path and rely on alcohol and sex and other such things to improve our lives! However, if there is a possibility of eliminating the inner enemy, then I think we should take the opportunity of having a human body, a human brain and a good human heart, and combine these strengths to reduce and ultimately uproot it. This is why human life is considered to be so precious according to the Buddhist teachings, for it alone enables a being to train and transform the mind, mainly by virtue of intelligence and reasoning.

Buddhists distinguish between two kinds of emotion. One type is without reason, and is just based on prejudice. Hatred is one of these. This sort of emotion will rely on superficial reasons, of course, such as 'this person has hurt me terribly', but deep down, if you pursue that reasoning further, you find it does not go very far. Emotions without proper reason are what we call negative emotions. The other kind of emotion, which includes compassion and altruism, is emotion with reason because through deep investigation you can prove it is good, necessary and useful. Furthermore, although by nature it is a type of emotion, it is actually in accord with reason and intelligence. In fact, it is by combining our intelligence and emotion that we can change and transform our inner world.

So long as the inner enemy is there, and so long as we are under its control, there can be no permanent happiness. Understanding the need to defeat this enemy is true realization, and developing a keen desire to overcome it is the aspiration to seek freedom, technically called renunciation. Therefore this practice of analysing our emotions and our inner world is very crucial.

The scriptures say that so far as the desire to overcome the first level of suffering is concerned, the 'suffering of suffering', even animals have it naturally. And so far as the aspiration to free oneself from the second level of suffering is concerned, the 'suffering of change', this is not something that is unique to the Buddhist path. Many ancient Indian non-Buddhist paths were similar, seeking inner tranquillity through samadhi. However, the genuine aspiration to seek complete liberation from samsara can only arise from a recognition of the third level of suffering, the 'suffering of conditioning', where we realize that so long as we remain under the control of ignorance we will be subject to suffering, and there will be no room for lasting joy and happiness. It may be said that the recognition of this third level of suffering is unique to the Buddhist path.

Questions

Q: Could Your Holiness please explain why the result of karma is sometimes instant and why on other occasions we have to wait lifetimes before the causal effect occurs?

HHDL: One factor would be the intensity of the karmic action itself. Another factor is the extent to which the various other conditions that are necessary for that karma to ripen are complete, and this is dependent, in turn, on other karmic actions. Vasubandhu addressed this issue in the Abhidharmakosha, in which he states that, generally speaking, the karmic actions which are the most forceful tend to produce their effects first. If the intensity of a karmic action is equal to that of another karmic action, then the result of the action with which the individual is most familiar tends to ripen first. However if two karmic actions are equally forceful and equally familiar, then the one that is committed earlier tends to produce its result first.

Q: Is there a difference between thought and action with regard to karmic effects? In other words, can a thought cause an action and vice versa?

HHDL: As I explained, the Buddhist concept of karma is not confined to bodily action alone; it also embraces mental acts, or we could say emotional acts. For example, when we talk about an act of covetousness, or a harmful intention, these are not necessarily manifest in behaviour. One could think such thoughts fully and in detail without expressing them in action at all, so a certain completion of these acts does happen on the mental level.

Furthermore, there are certain types of actions which do not necessarily have an immediate motivation or intention, but because of the conditioning from past karmic actions, one could have a propensity to act in a certain way. This means that some actions can arise not as a result of motivation, but as a result of karmic tendencies.

1. The term 'karma' comes from the Sanskrit word 'karman', meaning 'action'. It has three main meanings in Indian philosophy. The first is karma as ritual action, namely the sacrifice, in the early Vedas and Mimamsa philosophy. The second is karma as a particular category of human action, namely defiled and limited action, which we find in Samkhya Yoga, Advaita, the Bhagavad Gita and Buddhism. And the third meaning refers to karma not as an action but as a theory of action, in particular the theory of action as causal determinant. It is to this third meaning that the Dalai Lama refers here.

2. *Chatuhshatakashastrakarika,* chapter 8, verse 15.

3. See in particular the third and fourth chapters in Vasubandhu's *Abhidharmakosha.*

4. See a fuller discussion of this topic by His Holiness the Dalai Lama in dialogue with David Bohm in *Dialogues with Scientists and Sages: The Search for Unity,* edited by Renée Weber (Routledge and Kegan Paul, London, 1986).

four

The Truth of Cessation

The third Noble Truth is the Truth of Cessation. The key questions we must ask ourselves on this are the following: What is nirvana? What is *moksha* or liberation? What do we mean by *nirodha* or cessation? And is it really possible to attain cessation or not?

If we were to reply that we must accept that liberation is possible on the grounds that Buddha spoke of it in the scriptures, I don't think that is a satisfactory answer. It may be useful to reflect on a point that Aryadeva makes in his *Four Hundred Verses on the Middle Way*. He argues that when we talk about the ultimate nature of reality, or emptiness, we must realize that the understanding of emptiness is not something which requires reliance on scriptural authority. We can approach it through critical analysis and reasoning.

In Buddhism, we assert that one category of phenomena manifest to us and can be perceived directly, so there is no need for any logical proof of their existence. A second category of phenomena may not be obvious to us, but we can infer their existence through a process of reasoning. These are technically known as 'slightly obscure phenomena'. Emptiness belongs to this second category.[1]

Since we can infer the truth of emptiness, we must also accept that liberation can be inferred through the reasoning process too. As

Nagarjuna says, a true understanding of liberation should be based on an understanding of emptiness, because liberation is nothing other than the total elimination, or total cessation, of delusion and suffering through insight into emptiness. The concept of liberation is therefore very closely related to that of emptiness, and just as emptiness can be inferred, so can moksha.

On account of this intimate connection between emptiness and liberation in Buddhism, the passage in Maitreya's *Abhisamayalamkara* which deals with the third Noble Truth contains an extensive discussion of the 16 types of emptiness. The fact that liberation is an ultimate truth (and therefore related to emptiness) is explicitly discussed in Chandrakirti's writings as well. So it seems that our acceptance of liberation as a possibility is a function of how well we understand the concept of emptiness.

Emptiness
Four Interpretations of 'No-self' or Emptiness

When we talk about emptiness in Buddhism, it is clear that we are referring to the absence of something, a form of negation. In the same way the no-self theory is a form of negation. Why such insistence on categorical negation? Once again, let us pause for a while and consider our experience.

Let's imagine that I have a certain fear based on some kind of suspicion that there might be something threatening nearby. If the thought occurs to me that I may be mistaken, that it may be my projection, then although it will lessen my fear it will not completely dispel it. However, if instead I develop the thought that it is pure and utter illusion, that there isn't anything there at all and I'm just imagining it, and if my negation is that categorical, then of course it will have an immediate impact on dispelling my fear. The question is:

if that is the case, what is actually being negated? What is empty of what?

According to the scriptures, emptiness in this example is an absence of the object of negation, which in this case is the object of our fearful apprehension. This does not explain things fully, however, so we have to go further and try to understand what the object of negation actually is. The key to this question really lies in the way we understand the meaning of atman (self) in the context of anatman (no-self). Depending upon one's philosophical interpretation of the Buddha's teaching on anatman, there will be differences in the way one identifies what is being negated here.

Buddhist literature expresses varying degrees of subtlety concerning the identity of the atman as an object of negation. For instance, on one level[2] the atman is identified as substantially real, as a soul that exists within each one of us, and so in this context anatman means the negation of a substantially real, autonomous agent or eternal soul.

Then we have the interpretation of the Chittamatra school, which understands fundamental ignorance not as the belief in a substantially real and eternal soul, but rather as the belief in the reality of the physical world. The Chittamatrins understand fundamental ignorance, then, as the (erroneous) belief in the duality of mind and matter, so the object to be negated with respect to anatman is precisely this belief.

Thirdly, there is the Madhyamaka-Svatantrika understanding of emptiness. According to this school, although things come into being as a result of causes and conditions, and although the status of things as existing is in one sense or another dependent on our perception, nevertheless there is a certain intrinsic reality to things and events. What is negated by this school is the assertion that objects exist independent of perception, and it is this that constitutes their understanding of emptiness.

From the point of view of the Madhyamaka-Prasangika school, however, that is not the final meaning of the Buddha's teaching on anatman. According to this view, so long as we have not deconstructed or dismantled the notion that things and events can have any type of intrinsic existence whatsoever, then we are still grasping at things as real, as though they enjoyed some kind of independent status. Therefore the Prasangika-Madhyamikas negate the intrinsic existence and identity of things and events, and claim that *this* is the true meaning of emptiness.

Despite these differences, what all four schools have in common is a concern to emphasize that while we are rightly engaged in counteracting our grasping at the self, it is important to ensure that our negation does not defy the reality of the conventional world, the world of lived experience. There is a shared understanding that causality and the operation of karma should not be negated in the process. It seems that the Madhyamaka-Prasangika approach is the most successful in this respect, in so far as it uses a form of analysis that allows a thorough and complete negation of atman, while at the same time ensuring that the world of dependent origination and of karma is not destroyed but, on the contrary, re-affirmed.

The Middle Way

There is a very important passage[3] in Nagarjuna's *Fundamental Treatise on the Middle Way* (*Madhyamakamulakarika*), where he states: 'That which is dependently originated, I call empty. And that is, in turn, dependently designated.' The idea is that whatever is dependently originated is empty in the ultimate sense, and that what we designate, dependently, is nothing other than empty phenomena. The fact that things and events are dependently designated implies that they are not non-existent, they are not mere nothingness. So when an understanding of dependent origination is combined with an understanding of emptiness, we find that this enables an individual to tread the Middle Way, so-called because it avoids the extremes of absolutism and nihilism.

So the Madhyamaka expression 'dependently designated' has a deep significance. The first word, 'dependently', implies that things and events come into being through dependence on other factors, which means that they do not possess independent, autonomous, or absolute existence. So this first point negates absolutism. The second word, 'designated', implies that things and events are not mere nothingness, that they are not non-existent – that they do indeed exist. This part of the expression therefore ensures that the reality of the phenomenal world is not denied. As Buddhapalita states in his commentary on the *Fundamentals of the Middle Way*, if things and events have an independent existential status, and come into being without depending on other factors, then why are their designations dependent and interrelated?

In connection with this point, I have been told by various physicists that they are beginning to have problems in postulating an idea of reality that is in accordance with the quantum understanding of the physical world – even as a concept, reality is a problem. For me, this points to the difficulty of finding essences when we look into the essence of things. However, if we jump to the other extreme and say that everything is pure illusion and a mere projection of the mind, then we will be falling into the trap into which the Chittamatrins fell, namely the view of total mentalism. So if things do not possess intrinsic reality and yet, at the same time, if we are not happy with the conclusion that everything is a mere projection of the mind, what is the alternative? What is the middle way? The answer given by the Madhyamikas is that things and events arise purely as a result of the aggregation of many factors, and their conventional existence stems from the identity we impute to each aggregation.

As regards the exposition of the Buddhist doctrine of emptiness generally, we find there are many forms of reasoning presented in the literature which are designed to lead to an understanding of emptiness. Of all of these, the reasoning that is based on the understanding of dependent origination is considered to be the most effective. In order to develop the most profound understanding of the meaning of dependent origination, I think the works of Buddhapalita and Chandrakirti are crucial. Much of my own understanding and, naturally, most of the presentation I am making here, is based on Lama Tsongkhapa's exposition of these topics, which in turn is very much based on the reading of Nagarjuna by Chandrakirti and Buddhapalita, to the extent that Tsongkhapa substantiates almost every crucial point by referring to the commentaries of these two great masters.

When I study Nagarjuna's *Fundamentals of the Middle Way*, I combine the 23rd chapter dealing with the 12 links of dependent origination, with the 18th chapter on anatman. This latter chapter shows how it is the process of grasping at an eternal principle, or a substantially real soul, that binds us to unenlightened existence. It further shows how negating the principle of atman, and eliminating that grasping, lead to liberation. The main point is to underline how important it is to gain insight into emptiness.

I then combine my study of these two chapters with that of the 24th, in which Nagarjuna anticipates a number of the objections which could be put forward by the realist schools of Buddhism. The core of their objections could be summarized in this way: if there is no intrinsic reality, and if there is no intrinsic existence and identity to things and events, then there is no-thing. It follows that there cannot be any Four Noble Truths; if there are no Four Noble Truths there are no Three Jewels; if there are no Three Jewels there cannot be a Path to enlightenment. Nagarjuna responds by turning the realists' own criticism against them by saying that, on the contrary, if things do exist intrinsically then the consequences the realists attribute to his argument would apply to theirs. That is to say, if things are intrinsically real then the Four Noble Truths would not apply, nor could causes produce effects. So the central message of that chapter is to demonstrate that what Nagarjuna means by emptiness is not a mere nothingness, or a mere non-existence. Emptiness should be understood in terms of the interdependent nature of reality: it is by virtue of their dependent origination that things are devoid of independent existence.

Lodrö Gyatso, a Tibetan master from Amdo, captured this point in a beautiful verse.[4] He said that emptiness in this context does not mean the absence of functionality. What does it mean then? It is the emptiness of real or absolute existence. Dependent origination does not entail intrinsic reality or intrinsic identity, but what it does entail is illusion-like, phenomenal reality. So when you understand the meaning of both emptiness and dependent origination, you can posit emptiness and appearance simultaneously, within one locus, without contradiction.

Furthermore, the same master added that all philosophical schools describe their own position as avoiding the extreme of absolutism by talking about some form of emptiness, and avoiding the other extreme of nihilism by talking about the level of phenomenal reality. He pointed out, however, that it is only when you reverse the process that you overcome all forms of clinging: that is the Madhyamaka-Prasangika position, of course. From the point of view of Madhyamaka-Prasangika, then, it is through understanding appearance that a person is liberated from grasping onto absolutes, and it is by understanding the true meaning of emptiness that a person is freed from falling into nihilism.

The Madhyamaka Schools

Earlier I spoke about there being two different understandings of emptiness even within the Madhyamaka school itself, and I outlined how the Madhyamaka-Svatantrika view differs from that of the Madhyamaka-Prasangika. The basis for accepting this difference comes from the writings of Bhavaviveka, one of the chief disciples of Nagarjuna, who subjects the Buddhist realist schools to very critical examination, and at the same time criticizes Buddhapalita's reading of Nagarjuna. Bhavaviveka's own position emerges through these two critiques. In essence, he maintains that although they deny absolute existence, they do accept some form of intrinsic and objective reality to things and events, which Madhyamaka-Prasangika masters like Chandrakirti totally reject. So although Chandrakirti, Buddhapalita and Bhavaviveka were all great disciples of Nagarjuna, there is a substantial difference in their respective understanding of Nagarjuna's philosophy of emptiness. It is on account of this difference that Tibetan Buddhist scholars distinguish two divisions within the Madhyamaka school, which they call Svatantrika and Prasangika.

These two schools also differ in their methodology. The Madhyamaka-Prasangikas lay much greater emphasis on what is called the consequentialist style of reasoning. This resembles the *reductio ad absurdum* where you are not so much using reason to affirm something yourself, but rather you are concerned with showing the internal inconsistencies of your opponent's standpoint. In contrast, the Madhyamaka-Svatantrikas tend to use a syllogistic type of reasoning to establish their own positions.

Furthermore, there is another fundamental difference between Bhavaviveka and Chandrakirti which concerns the way our senses perceive material objects. For Bhavaviveka, it is valid to say that when a visual perception arises we see the appearance of an objective entity, because he accepts that things do possess a degree of objectivity which is then projected on to the perception. This is totally rejected by the Madhyamaka-Prasangika school of Chandrakirti. It is clear, therefore, that the central point of difference between the two Madhyamaka schools is whether or not one accepts any idea of intrinsicality.

Applying our Understanding of Emptiness

The reason why it is so important to understand this subtle point is because of its implications for interpreting our own personal experience of life. When strong emotions arise in you, say attachment or anger, if you examine the experience of that emotion you will see that underlying it is an assumption that there is something objective and real out there which you are holding on to, and on to which you project desirable or undesirable qualities. According to the kind of qualities you project on to a thing or event, you feel either attracted to it or repulsed by it. So strong emotional responses in fact assume the existence of some form of objective reality.

However, if you realize that there is no intrinsic reality to things and events then, of course, this will automatically help you to understand that no matter how real and strong emotions may seem, they have no valid basis. Once you know that they are actually based on a fundamental misconception of reality, then the emotions themselves become untenable. On the other hand, if your understanding of emptiness is not thorough, in the sense that you have not succeeded in negating the notion of intrinsicality completely, then of course your attitude towards emotion will be somewhat ambivalent, and you may feel that there is some sense in which it is valid or justified.

When you have developed a certain understanding of emptiness, albeit an intellectual one, you will have a new outlook on things and events which you can compare to your usual responses. You will notice how much we tend to project qualities on to the world. More especially, you will realise that most of our strong emotions arise from assuming the reality of something that is unreal. In this way you may be able to gain an experiential sense of the disparity between the way you perceive things and the way things really are. The moral that we can draw from all of this is that the strong emotions which afflict our mind arise from a fundamental state of confusion, which leads us to apprehend things as real and existing independently. In conclusion, we know that afflictive emotions and thoughts have no valid basis, neither in our experience, nor in reality, nor in reason.

By contrast, your insight into the emptiness of things is not only grounded in reason but also in experience: it has valid support. In addition, your understanding of emptiness and your grasping at things as real are directly opposed to one other, so one cancels the other out. Since they are opposing forces, and given that one has valid grounding whereas the other does not, the final conclusion we can draw is that the more we deepen our understanding of emptiness, and the greater the power of our insight becomes, the more we see through the deception of emotions, and consequently the weaker those emotions become. Indeed, we come to realize that strong afflictive emotions and thoughts, and their basis which is ignorance, can be weakened, while insight into emptiness can be enhanced.

Liberation

We have arrived at a point in our examination where we can conceivably accept that the power of delusions and of ignorance can be reduced, but the question remains as to whether it is at all possible to eliminate them completely and eradicate them from our minds. Some of the points in Maitreya's *Uttaratantra* may be very critical here. According to that text, our potential for knowledge is intrinsic to our consciousness and is an inherent, natural quality of our mind, whereas all those factors which afflict the mind are not an essential part of it. Mental afflictions are distinct from the essential nature of our mind, and are therefore called adventitious.

So when we talk about gaining the perfect wisdom of a buddha, we should not think that we need to create qualities in ourselves that are not there already, and acquire them from somewhere outside of us. Rather, we should see perfect buddha wisdom as a potential that is being realized. The defilements of the mind hamper the natural expression of that potential which is inherent in our consciousness. It is as if the capacity for unobstructed knowledge is there in our mind, but the defilements obscure and hinder it from being fully developed and expressed. However, once our understanding of the mind is informed by the idea that the essential nature of mind is pure luminosity and mere experience, or the sheer capacity to know. We can then conceive of the possibility of eliminating these afflictions completely.

To sum up, in this chapter we have followed the conceptual approach to the question of whether or not it is actually possible to attain liberation.

Finally, if we accept that liberation is possible, how exactly is it to be understood? In the scriptures, liberation is characterized in terms of four features. The first feature describes it as the true cessation of the continuum of afflictions. According to the second feature, liberation is true peace, the state of total tranquillity where the individual has attained complete freedom from all defilements of the mind. It is described in the third feature as totally satisfying, because one has reached ultimate satisfaction. Fourthly, it is described as definite emergence, in the sense that one has definitely emerged from the process of unenlightened existence.

1. The third category of phenomena are 'very obscure phenomena', which are beyond ordinary direct perception and logical inference. Generally, they can only be established on the basis of another's testimony or through scriptural authority.

2. This view is held in particular by the Shravakayana schools, especially the Vaibhasikas or Sarvastivadins, and the Sautrantikas.

3. Chapter XXIV, verse 18.

4. His Holiness is referring to a text known as *The Interwoven Praise* (sPal mar bstod pa), which is a commentary in verse on Tsongkhapa's famous *Praise to the Buddha for his teachings on Dependent Origination* (rTen 'brel bstod pa). Lodrö Gyatso was a late nineteenth century Gelug master from Amdo and was more widely known as Chone Lama Rinpoche.

five

The Truth of the Path

If we accept that liberation is an achievable goal, how is it possible to achieve it? This question brings us to the fourth Noble Truth, which deals with the true path.

According to the Madhyamaka explanation, the true path should be understood in terms of developing a direct intuitive realization of emptiness. This is because the intuitive realization of emptiness leads directly to the attainment of cessation. However, in order to have such a realization one must have a basis in single-pointed meditation, since this is what leads to an experiential knowledge of emptiness. The point at which an individual attains that experiential knowledge[1] is said to be the beginning of what is called the path of linking or path of preparation, and the point at which he gains direct intuitive realization of emptiness is called the path of seeing.

The experiential knowledge of emptiness must in turn be based on an intellectual understanding of emptiness, developed through inference. Indeed, without that, it is impossible to attain a meditatively-based experience of emptiness. That initial stage of developing intellectual understanding is part of what is known as the path of accumulation. The threshold of this path is the point where the practitioner develops a genuine aspiration to attain liberation – and this we consider to be the very beginning of the Buddhist Path.

The Shravakayana Path

Even before we embark upon the Path,[2] a great deal of preparation is necessary. To begin with, the most important practice is that of the three higher trainings: the trainings in morality (Skt. shila), concentration or meditation (Skt. samadhi), and wisdom or insight (Skt. prajña). The scriptures generally describe the transition from one stage to another in terms of a meditator's experience. It is important to understand, therefore, that the actual path on which the individual travels is that of his or her progressively deepening knowledge and realization of emptiness, technically known as the wisdom aspect of the path. Moreover, the wisdom that realizes emptiness must be developed within the context of the union of the single-pointedness of mind and penetrative insight, known as the union of shamatha and vipashyana.

In order to experience a union of these two, we have to develop shamatha first, for only this will enable us to channel our energy and concentration. Training in shamatha is therefore key. For it to be successful two factors must be present, namely the application of mindfulness and the application of mental alertness. These two capacities themselves will only develop successfully if our single-pointedness of mind is based on an ethically sound life, in which we apply discipline both to our attitude and to our way of life. This, of course, underlines the fundamental importance of morality. So now we can see how the three trainings are connected to each other.

All of these practices are common to both the Shravakayana and the Mahayana.

The Mahayana Path

We must now look at another important aspect of Buddhism, namely the way that the entire teaching of Buddha is founded on compassion. Compassion is the very foundation of the Dharma. The practice of enhancing our good heart and developing an altruistic mind is aimed at deepening our understanding of compassion, and invigorating the compassionate potential that exists within us. It is on the basis of profound compassion that we develop the altruistic aspiration to seek enlightenment for the benefit of all.

Traditionally this is called the generation of bodhichitta. What is bodhichitta? In Maitreya's *Abhisamayalamkara* bodhichitta is described as having two motivating factors: the first is genuine compassion towards all beings, and the second is recognition of the need to attain full enlightenment in order to fulfil the welfare of others. Indeed, to develop the altruistic mind of bodhichitta, it is not enough to have mere compassion. Bodhichitta must be based on a compassion which carries a sense of responsibility so that you are willing to take upon yourself the task of helping others.

This sense of responsibility will only arise if you have generated a spontaneous, genuine compassion which extends to all sentient beings without exception. This is universal compassion. It is called *mahakaruna* or 'great compassion' to distinguish it from ordinary compassion which is limited. However, this itself will not arise unless you have genuine insight into the nature of suffering, both your own suffering and that of others. You recognize your state of being one of suffering, then you will also feel a genuine empathy and connection with others. So far as gaining insight into the nature of suffering is concerned, reflection on the first Noble Truth, the Truth of Suffering, will assist you in deepening your insight.

For an altruistic practitioner, it is important to realize that attaining liberation for oneself alone is not enough. Not only is it individualistic, but even from the point of view of one's own path to perfection, it is not a state of full awakening.

It is therefore crucial to nurture our natural empathy and our sense of closeness with others. One of the methods described in the Buddhist scriptures for doing this is to imagine that all beings are your mothers, or someone else who is dear to you. You awaken the compassion you naturally feel for your mother or someone dear, and extend it to all other beings. In this way you develop a natural and spontaneous empathy. However, empathy cannot arise if your emotions towards others fluctuate due to the fact that you view some as enemies and others as friends. That discrimination has to be overcome first, and for this the practice of equanimity is fundamental.

A different method is presented by Shantideva in *The Guide to the Bodhisattva's Way of Life* (*Bodhicharyavatara*). He explains a way of cultivating genuine empathy by considering others as equal to oneself. For example, just as you personally wish to be happy and overcome suffering, others too have a similar desire, and just as you have the right to achieve this, so do they. With that sense of equality you reverse your self-centred perspective, putting yourself in others' shoes and relating to them as if they were dearer to you than you are to yourself.

According to the Tibetan tradition, these two different methods are combined and then meditated upon. Once you have gained even a simulated experience of the altruistic mind as a result of your reflection and meditation, then the custom is to stabilize and reinforce it by participating in a ceremony where you explicitly generate bodhichitta. This should then be followed by a keen desire to engage in the activities of a bodhisattva. According to tradition, the practitioner formally takes the vows of a bodhisattva at that point. The bodhisattva ideal, or the activities of a bodhisattva, are summed up in the Three Precepts: the first is the precept of refraining from negative actions;

the second is the precept of deliberately engaging in virtuous actions; and the third is the precept of helping others.

From the point of view of how causal practices lead to a resultant state, bodhisattva practices are also sometimes described in terms of the two accumulations: the accumulations of merit and wisdom. The two accumulations come together in the union of method and wisdom and, in the Buddhist path, should never be separated.

The Vajrayana Path

The profundity and sophistication of Tantra or Vajrayana stem from the practice of unifying method and wisdom. To put it very briefly, one of the unique features of the union of method and wisdom in the Vajrayana teachings is that the practitioner first subjects his or her perception of self and the world to an understanding of emptiness, and dissolves everything into emptiness. That cognition of emptiness is then visualized (imaginatively, of course, at the beginning) as the perfect form of a meditational deity. Next, you reflect on the non-substantial or empty nature of that deity. So within one instance of cognition, both method and wisdom are present and complete: there is visualization of a deity and at the same time an understanding of the empty nature of that deity.

Within the Vajrayana tradition there are four principal classes of tantra according to the Gelug, Sakya and Kagyu schools; these are Kriya tantra, Carya tantra, Yoga tantra, and Highest Yoga tantra (Anuttarayogatantra). The first two classes do not involve taking Vajrayana vows; it is in the Yoga tantra and Highest Yoga tantra that tantric vows are taken. The Highest Yoga tantra also has meditative practices which use various physiological elements, such as visualizing the energy channels of the body, the energies that flow within the channels, the 'subtle drops', and so on. In all of these various types of meditation the key is always the aspiration of bodhichitta and insight into emptiness. Without these two factors none of them would even be considered to be Buddhist practices.

However, in some very reliable and authentic texts belonging to Yogatantra, it is said that the Vajrayana path can also be based on the understanding of emptiness held by the Chittamatra school, not necessarily on that of the Madhyamaka. Despite this, I feel that if tantric practice is to be comprehensive, and if one is to attain full realization of the tantric path, an insight into emptiness based on the Madhyamaka is actually crucial.

Advice on Following the Buddhist Path

There are three pieces of advice I would like to share with you.

The first is to say that unless you are able to establish a firm grounding in the basic practices of the Buddhadharma, such as those I have outlined, then even the supposedly profound practices of the Vajrayana path will have no effect. The point is that for a practising Buddhist, it is really vital to develop an understanding of the Four Noble Truths, and to meditate upon them. Meditation should therefore be an essential part of your practice, and it is important to remember that it should include both shamatha and vipashyana.

Another important factor is your determination. You should not imagine that all these developments can take place within a few days or a few years; they may even take several aeons, so determination is evidently vital. If you consider yourself a Buddhist and want to really practise Buddhadharma, then right from the start you must make up your mind to do so until the end, regardless of whether it takes millions or billions of aeons. After all, what is the meaning of our life? In itself, there is no intrinsic meaning. However, if we use life in a positive way, then even the days and the months and the aeons can become meaningful. On the other hand, if you just fritter your life away aimlessly then even one day feels too long. You will find that once you have a firm determination and a clear objective, then time is not important.

As Shantideva writes in this beautiful prayer:

> For as long as space exists
> And sentient beings endure,
> May I too remain,
> To dispel the misery of the world.[3]

His words really convey a certain understanding to me, and they are so inspiring.

My final point is that the more impatient you are, and the more you want the way that is quickest, cheapest or best, the more likely you are to obtain a poor result. So I suggest this is the wrong approach.

Conclusion

If I were to essentialize my talk, I would say that if your understanding of the Four Noble Truths arises from deep reflections such as these, then you will gain a profound admiration for the Dharma, which is the true Refuge, and you will also develop a conviction in the possibility of actualizing the Dharma within yourself. On the basis of such a conviction you will be able to develop genuine devotion in the Buddha, the master who showed you the path, and you will also have a deep respect for the Sangha members who are your spiritual companions on the path.

If your understanding of the Three Jewels is based on a realization of the Four Noble Truths that is as profound as this, then whenever you think of Buddha, Dharma, and Sangha, they will come alive for you with renewed freshness. This is what is meant by Going for Refuge.

In fact, to summarize even more succinctly, the whole of the explanation I have given here is to show what is meant by Going for Refuge in the Three Jewels.

Although my own practice is very poor, very poor indeed, and although I recite mantras and visualize certain mandalas, even so the main emphasis of my daily practice is the Four Noble Truths and bodhichitta. These two practices I feel are of real practical benefit. Sometimes I think that visualizing deities can almost be like a way of deceiving oneself. In my view we must pursue practice step-by-step, with patience and determination. If you practise in this way, then after a year or after a decade you will notice at least some improvement in yourself, and when you see that, it brings a new encouragement to continue. However, we must realize that change is not at all easy.

So now you have read these teachings on the Four Noble Truths, if you consider you are a Buddhist then please put them into practice. They should not remain merely on an intellectual level. Practice and teaching must be part of our life. The same applies, of course, to practitioners and believers of other faiths, such as Christians, Muslims or Jews: whatever your faith, if you accept that faith then it must become part of your life. It is not sufficient to attend church on Sunday and join your hands together in prayer for a few moments, if the rest of your behaviour remains the same. Whether or not you are physically in a church or a cathedral, I think the teaching of your own religion must be in your heart. That's very important. Only then will you have an experience of it that is of real value, otherwise it is simply a piece of knowledge in your head and when you are faced with problems in life it won't be of any help.

Once the teaching is part of your life, whenever you have a real problem it gives you inner strength. Also, when you grow old, or have an incurable illness, and when death finally comes, then your practice truly gives you some kind of inner guarantee. After all, death is part of life; there is nothing strange about it; sooner or later we all have to pass through that gate. At that time, whether or not there is a life after, it is very valuable to have peace of mind. How can we achieve peace of mind at such a moment? It is possible only if we have some experience in ourselves that will provide inner strength, because no-one else can provide this for us – no deities, no gurus, and no friends. This is why Buddha says you must be your own master.

1. See the *Dasabhumika Sutra* for an explanation of the stages of the bodhisattva path.

2. In the Indian tradition, the Buddhist path was generally presented as the Noble Eightfold Path, which is composed of: right view, right intention, right speech, right action, right livelihood, right effort, right meditation, and right concentration. The Tibetan tradition also describes the Buddhist path in terms of the Five Paths, which are the path of accumulation, the path of connection, the path of seeing, the path of meditation, and the path of no more learning. Within this framework, the Noble Eightfold Path would be included in the path of meditation.

3. The Bodhicharyavatara by Shantideva, X.55.

Appendix

Compassion, the Basis for Human Happiness

*Public talk given by His Holiness the Dalai Lama
in the Free Trade Hall, Manchester, UK
19th July 1996*

I think that every human being has an innate sense of 'I'. We cannot explain why that feeling is there, but it is. Along with it comes a desire for happiness and a wish to overcome suffering. This is quite justified: we have a natural right to achieve as much happiness as possible, and we also have the right to overcome suffering.

The whole of human history has developed on the basis of this feeling. In fact it is not limited to human beings; from the Buddhist point of view, even the tiniest insect has this feeling and, according to its capacity, is trying to gain some happiness and avoid unhappy situations.

However, there are some major differences between human beings and other animal species. They stem from human intelligence. On account of our intelligence, we are much more advanced and have a greater capacity. We are able to think much further into the future, and our memory is powerful enough to take us back many years. Furthermore, we have oral and written traditions which remind us of events many centuries ago. Now, thanks to scientific methods, we can even examine events which occurred millions of years ago.

So our intelligence makes us very smart, but at the same time, precisely because of that fact, we also have more doubts and suspicions, and hence more fears. I think the imagination of fear is much more developed in humans than in other animals. In addition, the many conflicts within the human family and within one's own family, not to mention the conflicts within the community and between nations, as well as the internal conflicts within the individual – all conflicts and contradictions arise from the different ideas and views our intelligence brings. So unfortunately, intelligence can sometimes create a quite unhappy state of mind. In this sense, it becomes another source of human misery. Yet, at the same time, I think that ultimately intelligence is the tool with which we can overcome all these conflicts and differences.

From this point of view, of all the various species of animal on the planet, human beings are the biggest troublemakers. That is clear. I imagine that if there were no longer any humans on the planet, the planet itself would be safer! Certainly millions of fish, chicken and other small animals might enjoy some sort of genuine liberation!

It is therefore important that human intelligence be utilized in a constructive way. That is the key. If we utilize its capacity properly, then not only human beings would become less harmful to each other, and to the planet, but also individual human beings would be happier in themselves. It is in our hands. Whether we utilize our intelligence in the right way or the wrong way is up to us. Nobody can impose their values on us. How can we learn to use our capacity constructively? First, we need to recognize our nature and then, if we have the determination, there is a real possibility of transforming the human heart.

On this basis, I will speak today on how a human being can find happiness as an individual, because I believe the individual is the key to all the rest. For change to happen in any community, the initiative must come from the individual. If the individual can become a good, calm, peaceful person, this automatically brings a positive atmosphere to the family around him or her. When parents are warm-hearted, peaceful and calm people, generally speaking their children will also develop that attitude and behaviour.

The way our attitude works is such that it is often troubled by outside factors, so one side of the issue is to eliminate the existence of trouble around you. The environment, meaning the surrounding situation, is a very important factor for establishing a happy frame of mind. However, even more important is the other side of the issue, which is one's own mental attitude.

The surrounding situation may not be so friendly, it may even be hostile, but if your inner mental attitude is right, then the situation will not disturb your inner peace. On the other hand, if your attitude is not right, then even if you are surrounded by good friends and the best facilities, you cannot be happy. This is why mental attitude is more important than external conditions. Despite this, it seems to me that many people are more concerned about their external conditions, and neglect the inner attitude of mind. I suggest that we should pay more attention to our inner qualities.

There are a number of qualities which are important for mental peace, but from the little experience I have, I believe that one of the most important factors is human compassion and affection: a sense of caring.

Let me explain what we mean by compassion. Usually, our concept of compassion or love refers to the feeling of closeness we have with our friends and loved ones. Sometimes compassion also carries a sense of pity. This is wrong – any love or compassion which entails looking down on the other is not genuine compassion. To be genuine, compassion must be based on respect for the other, and on the realisation that others have the right to be happy and overcome suffering just as much as you. On this basis, since you can see that others are suffering, you develop a genuine sense of concern for them.

As for the closeness we feel towards our friends, this is usually more like attachment than compassion. Genuine compassion should be unbiased. If we only feel close to our friends, and not to our enemies, or to the countless people who are unknown to us personally and towards whom we are indifferent, then our compassion is only partial or biased.

As I mentioned before, genuine compassion is based on the recognition that others have the right to happiness just like yourself, and therefore even your enemy is a human being with the same wish for happiness as you, and the same right to happiness as you. A sense of concern developed on this basis is what we call compassion; it extends to everyone, irrespective of whether the person's attitude towards you is hostile or friendly.

One aspect of this kind of compassion is a sense of caring responsibility. When we develop that kind of motivation, our self-confidence increases automatically. This in turn reduces fear, and that serves as a basis for determination. If you are really determined right from the beginning to accomplish a difficult task, then even if you fail first time, second time, third time, it doesn't matter. Your aim is very clear, so you will continue to make an effort. This sort of optimistic and determined attitude is a key factor for success.

Compassion also brings us a certain inner strength. Once it is developed, it naturally opens an inner door, through which we can communicate with other fellow human beings, and even other sentient beings, with ease, and heart to heart. On the other hand, if you feel hatred and ill-feeling towards others, they may feel similarly towards you, and as a result suspicion and fear will automatically create a distance between you and make communication difficult. You will then feel lonely and isolated. Not all members of your community will have similar negative feelings towards you, but some may look on you negatively because of your own feeling.

If you harbour negative feelings towards others, and yet expect them to be friendly to you, you are being illogical. If you want the atmosphere around you to be more friendly, you must first create the basis for that. Whether the response of others is positive or negative, you must first create the ground of friendliness. If others still respond to you negatively after this, then you have the right to act accordingly.

I always try to create a ground of friendliness with people. Whenever I meet someone new, for example, I feel no need for introductions. The person is obviously another human being. Maybe sometime in the future, technological advances may mean that I could confuse a robot for a human being, but up to now this has never happened. I see a smile, some teeth and eyes, and so on, and I recognize the person as a human being! On that basis, on the emotional level we are the same, and basically on the physical level we are the same, except for colouring. But whether Westerners have yellow hair, or blue hair, or white hair, does not really matter. The important thing is that we are the same on the emotional level. With that conviction, I feel that the other person is a human brother, and approach him spontaneously. In most cases, the other person immediately responds accordingly, and becomes a friend. Sometimes I fail, and then I have the liberty to react according to the circumstances.

Basically, therefore, we should approach others openly, recognizing each person as another human being just like ourselves. There is not so much difference between us all.

Compassion naturally creates a positive atmosphere, and as a result you feel peaceful and content. Wherever there lives a compassionate person, there is always a pleasant atmosphere. Even dogs and birds approach the person easily. Almost fifty years ago, I used to keep some birds in the Norbulingka Summer Palace, in Lhasa. Among them was a small parrot. At that time I had an elderly attendant whose appearance was somewhat unfriendly – he had very round, stern eyes – but he was always feeding this parrot with nuts and so on. So whenever the attendant would appear, just the sound of his footsteps or his coughing would mean the parrot would show some excitement. The attendant had an extraordinarily friendly manner with that small bird, and the parrot also had an amazing response to him. On a few occasions I fed him some nuts but he never showed such friendliness to me, so I started to poke him with a stick, hoping he might react differently; the result was totally negative. I was using more force than the bird had, so it reacted accordingly.

Therefore, if you want a genuine friend, first you must create a positive atmosphere around you. We are social animals, after all, and friends are very important. How can you bring a smile to people's faces? If you remain stony and suspicious, it is very difficult. Perhaps if you have power or money, some people may offer you an artificial smile, but a genuine smile will only come from compassion.

The question is how to develop compassion. In fact, can we really develop this unbiased compassion at all? My answer is that we definitely can. I believe that human nature is gentle and compassionate, although many people, both in the past and now, think that human nature is basically aggressive. Let us examine this point.

At the time of conception, and while we are in our mother's womb, our mother's compassionate and peaceful mental state is a very positive factor for our development. If the mother's mind is very agitated, it is harmful for us. And that is just the beginning of life! Even the parents' state of mind at conception itself is important. If a child is conceived through rape, for example, then the child will be unwanted, which is a terrible thing. For conception to take place properly, it should come from genuine love and mutual respect, not just mad passion. It is not enough to have some casual love affair, the two partners should know each other well and respect each other as people, and this is the basis for a happy marriage. Furthermore, marriage itself should be for life, or at least should be long lasting. Life should properly start from such a situation.

Then, according to medical science, in the few weeks after birth, the child's brain is still growing. During that period, the experts claim that physical touch is a crucial factor for the proper development of the brain. This alone shows that the mere growth of our body requires another's affection.

After birth, one of the first acts on the mother's side is to give milk, and from the child's side it is to suckle. Milk is often considered a symbol of compassion. Without it, traditionally the child cannot survive. Through the process of suckling there comes a closeness between mother and child. If that closeness is not there, then the child will not seek its mother's breast, and if the mother is feeling dislike towards the child her milk may not come freely. So milk comes with affection. This means that the first act of our life, that of taking milk, is a symbol of affection. I am always reminded of this when I visit a church and see Mary carrying Jesus as a small baby; that to me is a symbol of love and affection.

It has been found that those children who grow up in homes where there is love and affection have a healthier physical development and study better at school. Conversely, those who lack human affection have more difficulty in developing physically and mentally. These children also find it difficult to show affection when they grow up, which is such a great tragedy.

Now let us look at the last moment of our lives – death. Even at the time of death, although the dying person can no longer benefit much from his friends, if he is surrounded by friends his mind may be more calm. Therefore throughout our lives, from the very beginning right up to our death, human affection plays a very important role.

An affectionate disposition not only makes the mind more peaceful and calm, but it affects our body in a positive way too. On the other hand, hatred, jealousy and fear upset our peace of mind, make us agitated and affect our body adversely. Even our body needs peace of mind, and is not suited to agitation. This shows that an appreciation of peace of mind is in our blood.

Therefore, although some may disagree, I feel that although the aggressive side of our nature is part of life, the dominant force of life is human affection. This is why it is possible to strengthen that basic goodness which is our human nature.

We can also approach the importance of compassion through intelligent reasoning. If I help another person, and show concern for him or her, then I myself will benefit from that. However, if I harm others, eventually I will be in trouble. I often joke, half sincerely and half seriously, saying that if we wish to be truly selfish then we should be wisely selfish rather than foolishly selfish. Our intelligence can help to adjust our attitude in this respect. If we use it well, we can gain insight as to how we can fulfil our own self-interest by leading a compassionate way of life. It would even be possible to argue that being compassionate is ultimately selfish.

In this context, I do not think that selfishness is wrong. Loving oneself is crucial. If we do not love ourselves, how can we love others? It seems that when some people talk of compassion, they have the notion that it entails a total disregard for one's own interests – a sacrificing of one's interests. This is not the case. In fact genuine love should first be directed at oneself.

There are two different senses of self. One has no hesitation in harming other people, and that is negative and leads to trouble. The other is based on determination, will-power and self-confidence, and that sense of 'I' is very necessary. Without it, how can we develop the confidence we need to carry out any task in life? Similarly, there are two types of desire also. However, hatred is invariably negative and destructive of harmony.

How can we reduce hatred? Hatred is usually preceded by anger. Anger rises as a reactive emotion, and gradually develops into a feeling of hatred. The skilful approach here is first to know that anger is negative. Often people think that as anger is part of us, it is better to express it, but I think this is misguided. You may have grievances or resentment due to your past, and by expressing your anger you might be able to finish with them. That is very possible. Usually, however, it is better to check your anger, and then gradually, year by year, it diminishes. In my experience, this works best when you adopt the position that anger is negative and it is better not to feel it. That position itself will make a difference.

Whenever anger is about to come, you can train yourself to see the object of your anger in a different light. Any person or circumstance which causes anger is basically relative; seen from one angle it makes you angry, but seen from another perspective you may discover some good things in it. We lost our country, for example, and became refugees. If we look at our situation from that angle, we might feel frustration and sadness, yet the same event has created new opportunities – meeting with other people from different religious traditions, and so on. Developing a more flexible way of seeing things helps us cultivate a more balanced mental attitude. This is one method.

There are other situations where you might fall sick, for example, and the more you think about your sickness the worse your frustration becomes. In such a case, it is very helpful to compare your situation with the worst case scenario related to your illness, or with what would have happened if you had caught an even more serious illness, and so on. In this way, you can console yourself by realizing that it could have been much worse. Here again, you train yourself to see the relativity of your situation. If you compare it with something that is much worse, this will immediately reduce your frustration.

Similarly, if difficulties come they may appear enormous when you look at them closely, but if you approach the same problem from a wider perspective, it appears smaller. With these methods, and by developing a larger outlook, you can reduce your frustration whenever you face problems. You can see that constant effort is needed, but if you apply it in this way, then the angry side of you will diminish. Meanwhile, you strengthen your compassionate side and increase your good potential. By combining these two approaches, a negative person can be transformed into a kind one. This is the method we use to effect that transformation.

In addition, if you have religious faith, it can be useful in extending these qualities. For example, the Gospels teach us to turn the other cheek, which clearly shows the practice of tolerance. For me, the main message of the Gospels is love for our fellow human beings, and the reason we should develop this is because we love God. I understand this in the sense of having infinite love. Such religious teachings are very powerful to increase and extend our good qualities. The Buddhist approach presents a very clear method. First, we try to consider all sentient beings as equal. Then we consider that the lives of all beings are just as precious as our own, and through this we develop a sense of concern for others.

What of the case of someone who has no religious faith? Whether we follow a religion or not is a matter of individual right. It is possible to manage without religion, and in some cases it may make life simpler! But when you no longer have any interest in religion, you should not neglect the value of good human qualities. As long as we are human beings, and members of human society, we need human compassion. Without that, you cannot be happy. Since we all want to be happy, and to have a happy family and friends, we have to develop compassion and affection. It is important to recognize that there are two levels of spirituality, one with religious faith, and one without. With the latter, we simply try to be a warm-hearted person.

We should also remember that once we cultivate a compassionate attitude, non-violence comes automatically. Non-violence is not a diplomatic word, it is compassion in action. If you have hatred in your heart, then very often your actions will be violent, whereas if you have compassion in your heart, your actions will be non-violent.

As I said earlier, as long as human beings remain on this Earth there will always be disagreements and conflicting views. We can take that as given. If we use violence in order to reduce disagreements and conflict, then we must expect violence every day and I think the result of this is terrible. Furthermore, it is actually impossible to eliminate disagreements through violence. Violence only brings even more resentment and dissatisfaction.

Non-violence, on the other hand, means dialogue, it means using language to communicate. And dialogue means compromise: listening to others' views, and respecting others' rights, in a spirit of reconciliation. Nobody will be 100 per cent winner, and nobody will be 100 per cent loser. That is the practical way. In fact, that is the only way.

Today, as the world becomes smaller and smaller, the concept of 'us' and 'them' is almost out-dated. If our interests existed independently of those of others, then it would be possible to have a complete winner and a complete loser, but since in reality we all depend on one another, our interests and those of others are very interconnected. So how can you gain 100 per cent victory? It is impossible. You have to share, half-half, or if at all possible 60 per cent this side and 40 per cent the other side! Without this approach, reconciliation is impossible.

The reality of the world today means that we need to learn to think in this way. This is the basis of my own approach – the 'middle way' approach. Tibetans will not be able to gain 100 per cent victory for whether we like it or not, the future of Tibet very much depends on China. Therefore, in the spirit of reconciliation, I advocate a sharing of interests so that genuine progress is possible. Compromise is the only way. Through non-violent means we can share views, feelings, and rights, and in this way we can solve the problem.

I sometimes call the 20th century a century of bloodshed, a century of war. Over this century there have been more conflicts, more bloodshed and more weapons than ever before. Now, on the basis of the experience we have all had this century, and of what we have learned from it, I think we should look to the next century to be one of dialogue. The principle of non-violence should be practised everywhere. This cannot be achieved simply by sitting here and praying. It means work and effort, and yet more effort.

Thank you.

Glossary

Abhidharmakosha *(Treasury of Knowledge) by Vasubandhu. English translation (from a French translation) by Leo M. Pruden,* Abhidharmakoshabhashyam, *Berkeley, California, Asian Humanities Press, 1991.*

Abhidarmasamuchchaya *– see Compendium of Knowledge*

Arhat *(Tib. dgra bcom pa) – to become an Arhat is the final goal of the Shravakayana. It is a form of nirvana, beyond rebirth, but falls short of buddhahood. The Tibetan word literally means 'one who has subdued the enemies', i.e. negative emotions.*

Aryadeva *– a disciple of Nagarjuna and author of many important commentaries.*

Asanga *– great fourth century Indian master, half-brother of Vasubandhu, who composed important Mahayana works inspired by Maitreya. He is especially known as a proponent of the Cittamatra school.*

Bhavaviveka *– also known as Bhavya, the key figure in the development of Svatantrika-Madhyamaka.*

Bodhicharyavatara *– see Guide to the Bodhisattva's Way of Life.*

Bodhisattva *– a being who has decided to bring all beings to enlightenment and who is practising the Bodhisattva path of the Mahayana.*

Buddhapalita *– circa 4th century Indian master, founder of Prasangika-Madhyamaka.*

Chandrakirti – *circa 3–4th century master, the greatest figure in the Prasangika-Madhyamaka school.*

Chatuhshatakashastrakarika – *see* Four Hundred Verses on the Middle Way

Clear Words *(abbreviated Skt. title: Prasannapada; full title: Mulamadhyamakavrttiprasannapada) – a commentary by Chandrakirti on Nagarjuna's Mulamadhyamikakarika. English translation of selected chapters in M. Sprung, 'Lucid Exposition of the Middle Way'.*

Commentary on the Compendium of Valid Cognition *by Dharmakirti.*

Compendium of Knowledge *(Abhidarmasamuchchaya) by Asanga. French translation by Walpola Rahula,* Le Compendium de la Super-Doctrine *(Philosophie d'Asanga), Paris, Ecole Française d'Extrême-Orient, 1971.*

Dharmakirti – *famous Buddhist logician of the 7th century.*

Emptiness *(Skt. shunyata) – the absence of true existence in all phenomena.*

Enlightenment *(Skt. bodhi) – purification of all obscurations and realization of all qualities.*

Four Hundred Verses on the Middle Way *(Chatuhshatakashastrakarika) by Aryadeva. English translations by K. Lang,* Aryadeva's Catuhsataka: On the Bodhisattva's Cultivation of Merit and Knowledge, Indiske Studier, Vol. VII, Copenhagen, Akademish Forlag, 1986; *and Geshe Sonam Rinchen and Ruth Sonam,* Yogic Deeds of the Bodhisattvas: Gyelstap on Aryadeva's Four Hundred, Ithaca, Snow Lion, 1994.

Fundamentals of the Middle Way *(Mulamadhyamikakarika) – a seminal text by Nagarjuna. English translation by F. Streng,* Emptiness: A Study in Religious Meaning, Nashville and New York, Abingdon Press, 1967. See also K. Inada, Nagarjuna: A Translation of his Mulamadhyamikakarika, Tokyo, Hokuseido Press, 1970.

Guide to the Bodhisattva's Way of Life (*Bodhicharyavatara*) *by Shantideva. English translations include* A Guide to the Bodhisattva's Way of Life *by Stephen Batchelor, Dharamsala, Library of Tibetan Works and Archives, 1979.*

Liberation (*skt. moksha*) – *freedom from samsara, either as an arhat or as a buddha.*

Madhyamaka – *literally 'the middle way'. The highest of the four main Buddhist schools of philosophy. First expounded by Nagarjuna and considered to be the basis of Vajrayana. The Middle Way means not holding to any extreme views, especially those of eternalism and nihilism.*

Mahayana – *literally 'the Great Vehicle', the vehicle of bodhisattvas. It is great because it aims at full buddhahood for the sake of all beings. These teachings take the cause as path.*

Maitreya – *the Buddha to come, the fifth in this present cosmic age. Many Mahayana teachings were inspired by Maitreya.*

Mandala – *the universe with the palace of a deity in the centre, as described in the Tantric practice of visualisation.*

Mantra – *manifestation of supreme enlightenment in the form of sound. Syllables used in Tantric visualisation practices to invoke the wisdom deities.*

Mulamadhyamikakarika – *see Fundamentals of the Middle Way*

Nagarjuna – *Indian master of 1st–2nd century* CE *who expounded the teachings of Madhyamaka, and composed numerous philosophical and medical treatises.*

Path of accumulation – *the first of the five paths according to Mahayana. On this path one accumulates the causes that will make it possible to proceed towards enlightenment.*

Path of connection – *the second of the five paths according to Mahayana. On this path one connects oneself to, or prepares oneself for,* *seeing the two kinds of absence of self.*

Path of seeing – *the third of the five paths according to Mahayana. It is called this because one really sees the two kinds of absence of self, that of the individual and that of phenomena.*

Pramanavarttikakarika – *see Commentary on the Compendium of Valid Cognition.*

Prasannapada – *see Clear Words.*

Samsara – *the cycle of unenlightened existence in which one is endlessly propelled by negative emotions and karma from one state of rebirth to another. The root of Samsara is ignorance.*

Shamatha – *'calm abiding'. The meditative practice of calming the mind in order to rest free from the disturbance of thought.*

Shantideva – *great Indian poet and master of the 7th century CE, who lived at the famous Nalanda University.*

Shravaka – *follower of the root vehicle of Buddhism (Shravakayana) whose goal is to attain liberation from the suffering if samsara as an arhat. Unlike bodhisattvas, shravakas do not aspire to attain enlightenment for the sake of all beings.*

Shravakayana – *the vehicle of the hearers or listeners, based on the teachings of the Four Noble Truths.*

Sutra – *the teachings of both the Shravakayana and the Mahayana.*

Uttaratantra – *the full Sanskrit title is Mahayana-uttaratantrashastra (Supreme Continuum of the Mahayana). This text is ascribed to Maitreya. English translations from the Sanskrit by E. Obermiller,* Sublime Science of the Great Vehicle to Salvation *in* Acta Orientalia *9 (1931), pp. 81–306; and J. Takasaki,* A Study on the Ratnagotravibhaga, *Rome, ISMEO, 1966. English translation from the Tibetan by Ken and Katia Holmes,* The Changeless Nature, *Dumfriesshire, Karma Drubgyud Darjay Ling, 1985.*

Vajrayana – *literally 'the diamond vehicle', also known as Tantrayana.*

These teachings take the result as path.

Vasubandhu – *great fourth century Indian master, brother of Asanga, who composed classic philosophical works on the Sarvastivada, Sautrantika and Cittamatra doctrines.*

Vipashyana – *clear insight meditation.*

Recommended Reading

The Dalai Lama, *The World of Tibetan Buddhism* (translated by Thubten Jinpa), Wisdom, Boston, 1995

The Dalai Lama, *The Meaning of Life from a Buddhist Perspective* (translated and edited by Jeffrey Hopkins), Wisdom, 1992

Jeremy Hayward and Francisco J Varela (eds), *Gentle Bridges Conversations with the Dalai Lama on the Sciences of the Mind*, Shambhala, USA, 1992

Geshe Lhundup Sopa and Jeffrey Hopkins (eds), *Cutting Through Appearances: Practice and Theory of Tibetan Buddhism*, Snow Lion, New York, 1989

Jamgön Kongtrul, *Myriad World*, Snow Lion, 1995

H.H. Dilgo Khyentse Rinpoche, *Pure Appearance: Development and Completion Stages in Vajrayana Practice*, Snow Lion, 1996